"Nobody fills our lives like Jesus and nobody loves us like Jesus. Jud Wilhite does an incredible job of clearing the way so that we can experience him more completely in *Empty No More*. This remarkable book will lead you back to the satisfaction found only in Jesus' radical love."

Pete Wilson, author of *Empty Promises*;
founding and senior pastor of Cross Point Church

"In *Empty No More*, Jud Wilhite delivers profoundly by showing how Jesus gives significance and value to our lives. This book could save you thousands on therapy and years of searching for what only God can provide."

Mike Foster, author of *Gracenomics*;
co-founder of People of the Second Chance

"After reading *Empty No More*, my life will never be the same—and neither will yours. This is the book I've been waiting to read my entire life, and Jud Wilhite has finally written it."

Pat Williams, senior vice president, Orlando Magic;
author of *How to Be Like Jesus*

empty no more

empty no more

EXPERIENCE THE
FULFILLING LOVE OF JESUS

jud wilhite

BakerBooks
a division of Baker Publishing Group
Grand Rapids, Michigan

Published by Baker Books
a division of Baker Publishing Group
P.O. Box 6287, Grand Rapids, MI 49516-6287
www.bakerbooks.com

Original edition published in 2003 under the title *Love That Goes the Distance: Discover the Power That Conquers All*

Printed in the United States of America

Library of Congress Cataloging-in-Publication Data
Wilhite, Jud, 1971–
    Empty no more : experience the fulfilling love of Jesus / Jud Wilhite.
        p.   cm.
    Rev. ed. of: Love that goes the distance.
    Includes bibliographical references (p.   ).
    ISBN 978-0-8010-1486-4 (pbk.)
    1. Love—Religious aspects—Christianity. I. Wilhite, Jud, 1971– Love that goes the distance. II. Title.
BV4639.W482 2012
241'.4—dc23   2012023272

To protect the privacy of those who have shared their stories with the author, some details and names have been changed.

The internet addresses, email addresses, and phone numbers in this book are accurate at the time of publication. They are provided as a resource. Baker Publishing Group does not endorse them or vouch for their content or permanence.

12   13   14   15   16   17   18   7   6   5   4   3   2   1

To Jim and Shawn

contents

acknowledgments

I am grateful to the many people who made an impact in my life and this book. I want to especially thank:

Dianna Melson, Michael Murphy, Paul Mudd—for lending your expertise and insight.

Chad Allen and everyone at Baker—for being both professional and dedicated.

Everyone who shared their personal stories for this project—your pain and victories inspire us all.

Lori, Emma, and Ethan—for who you are and all you mean to me.

introduction

ALL YOU CAN EAT

We're not in the business of filling bellies. We want to fill souls.

Howard Shultz, CEO of Starbucks

One benefit of living in the Las Vegas area is the buffets. Vegas is world famous for cheap buffets, although nowadays they aren't quite as cheap as they used to be. Every major establishment has one, and they're always busy. And it's easy to see why. For one price you get unlimited access to all kinds of different food. If you go to one of the mega-buffets, like the Carnival World Buffet at the Rio, you can literally get food from all different parts of the world. On one plate you can have fried chicken, couscous, and egg foo yong. In a word, it's simply . . . *remarkable*.

The way I attack a buffet is like this: the first time through, I get a little bit of everything that looks good. Then I take it back to the table and taste it. If I like something, I go back

13

and get more of it. If I don't like it, I let the nice people take the plate away. Because hey . . . it's a buffet! You get *all* of what you *do* want, and *none* of what you *don't* want. Buffets are easier on the finances and tougher on the waistline—but no matter how much I eat, I'm still hungry the next morning.

One thing I've noticed, especially in recent years, is more and more people are taking a buffet approach to faith. America is like one big buffet line of religion. We can be tempted to take a little of what Jesus said here, a little of the Beatles over there, and mix in some Oprah, a few Buddhist nuggets, and some no-nonsense Dr. Phil and Dr. Drew life coaching. Before we know it we have our own self-made religion, buffet style. It's perfect, right? *All* of what we *do* want, and *none* of what we *don't* want.

The problem is that it isn't very satisfying in the end. We reduce faith not only to a personal thing, but to a completely individualized thing that in the end has little to do with true Christianity. We've simply made God in our image. The outcome is frustration and dissatisfaction.

I've experienced the buffet tendency in my own faith as a committed Christian and pastor. I gravitate to certain Bible passages and exclude others that make me feel uncomfortable. I relate to God out of my own self-centeredness and I don't allow him into the deeper places of my life to really heal me from the inside out. I make room enough for God on my terms, not his. I welcome him with one hand and give him the Heisman trophy move with the other. I allow the culture to influence my view of Jesus more than the Bible. I would never say that I am taking an *intentional* buffet approach to faith, but often I am nonetheless. And then I get discouraged when things don't feel like they are working, and I feel empty because I've settled for cheap imitations and half-truths.

Maybe you can relate. Perhaps you have developed a certain thought process about God and life that leaves you with a lingering sense of insignificance. You love him and trust that he is present in your life, but you just can't seem to connect all the dots. You've been hurt in the past and feel let down by God. Perhaps you've allowed a wall to build up in your heart toward him. Maybe God didn't come through with a work opportunity or a relationship despite all your prayers and hopes. Maybe you've come to find a certain familiarity in your pain that keeps you in a holding pattern despite your longing to move forward. Despite all your effort and objections to the contrary, in the quiet moments you still feel empty and burnt out, in need of encouragement.

Most of our beliefs about life and faith come from a myriad of sources ranging from our childhood, our playground experiences, our upbringing, our music and movie tastes, and our textbooks and yearbooks and ebooks. It is easy to simply morph God into all of this in a huge mash-up of faith. But the problem with the buffet is we are still empty in the end, and we don't know why. We've come to *believe* in Jesus, but we've stopped short of really *experiencing* Jesus' fulfilling love.

Jesus is so much more than our cultural mash-up has led us to believe. If we look at TV and movies, there are lots of perceptions about Jesus. Try to get a visual in your mind and you may think of Jim Caviezel from Mel Gibson's film *The Passion of the Christ.* I've met Jim and he's a nice guy, but he'd be the first to tell you he's no Jesus. On the other end of the spectrum is the "Buddy Christ" statue from the film *Dogma.* Buddy Christ is like a genie in a bottle who answers all of your prayers in the affirmative and doesn't really ask much of you. He's a Facebook friend who "likes" all of your photos, status updates, and links, but you don't ever really submit to his teachings. He is just a Buddy Christ who gives you a thumbs-up or fist-bump.

On *South Park* Jesus hosts his own TV show, *Jesus and Pals*. Kanye West rapped about how Jesus walks with rappers, drug dealers, and strippers. Carrie Underwood asked Jesus to take the wheel. And of course the Doobie Brothers sang that "Jesus is just all right with me." We've had sightings of Jesus on everything from grilled cheese sandwiches to dental X-rays to plaster walls. It is one huge buffet of perspectives, but it often leaves us confused and frustrated.

One way I defy the buffet approach to faith is to go back to the Bible and particularly the life of Jesus. By revisiting his interactions with others I learn about the way he wants to interact with me. By studying his teaching I'm convicted to take life on God's terms. I'm confronted with a God who loves me more than I could ever comprehend. And as I grow in this love I overflow with the significance that only comes from him.

In *Empty No More* I'll share how Jesus can shatter our false beliefs and assumptions and reveal how his love can fulfill us. I'll encourage you to:

Discover how Jesus' love can fulfill your deepest longings so that you are not spiritually famished.

Allow Jesus to heal your brokenness so that you can live as a more complete person.

Rediscover purpose for your life and feel satisfied in your calling.

Bridge the gap between the life you want and the one you're experiencing so that you're free to be yourself in Christ.

Jesus longs to teach us that his love is what we need in life's dilemmas. We don't have to hurt alone. We don't have to carry our burdens alone. We don't have to heal alone. Jesus, the great wounded healer, offers us something better than medicine, stronger than anesthesia, more powerful than antibiotics. He offers himself, his church, and his love. And as we'll see, he is more than enough.

1

hunger games

You don't forget the face of the person who was your last hope.

Suzanne Collins, *The Hunger Games*

I recently had the opportunity to go back to my childhood home. Stirred by the adult desire to understand all that had taken place there, I was visiting the vicinity, and I experienced a surge of homesickness as intense as when I'd been a kid at summer camp.

My parents had moved years earlier, but the current owners were kind enough to let me do a walk-through. The house was a straightforward single-story red brick with gray siding that my dad had painstakingly painted. It had a big front yard overshadowed by a large tree I had planted with him when I was a kid. I checked out the living room (same tan carpet) and concrete storm basement (my last name still visible in black permanent marker on the bottom of an old folding chair). I remembered playing in the backyard, the trees with the branches from which I'd swung and fallen, and the woodpile where I'd pretended to be Superman, leaping from the top to fly. But the most important moment in touring the house was standing in my former bedroom.

The room itself looked so much smaller than I remembered it, with two windows and off-white walls. I visualized my old posters of Twisted Sister and Ozzy Osborne pinned crookedly on the wall and noted where my cassette tape stereo (remember those?) used to sit. I recalled my old ceiling fan that tilted slightly and squeaked when it ran, like a plane propeller about to come off. I inspected the front window, from which I had snuck out way too many nights.

Then I looked at the floor in the center of the room where as a teenager I had prayed to God on my knees and surrendered my life to him. There was nothing special about it; it was just a bedroom floor. Yet standing in the room where I had received the gift of God's grace more than twenty years before was a powerful gift. I paused and whispered a prayer of thanks. I remembered where I came from.

Returning to my old bedroom reminded me that all my efforts to change and find contentment and freedom on my own had failed by the time God grabbed hold of me. What fundamentally changed me was a sustaining relationship with the living God. This bond was not based on me and what I had done, but on him and what he had done for me in relation to the gift of his son Jesus. He filled my life and gave it meaning.

Hunger Pains

My journey home recalibrated my heart toward Jesus as the only one who can satisfy my longings. Too often I had played my own type of hunger games—not physical hunger or survival games like *The Hunger Games* novel, but *spiritual* hunger games. Like everyone else, I desired to be fulfilled and to experience joy, to feel significance and to live with a sense of contentment. I *believed* God was the one who could provide these things, but I *acted* like everything but God would fill my life. I opted for the temporary distraction of entertainment rather than spending much-needed time with God. I gave myself over to more religious work as a pastor, but I wasn't personally engaging in my journey with God. I lived like a full-time pastor and a semi-retired Christian! After several years of these games I woke up one day and realized that spiritually I felt like an old abandoned motel with a "Vacancy" sign out front.

Maybe you've been playing your own hunger games. You're still trying to look the part, but inside you're dying. You hide your pain or questions behind a convincing smile, but you've got nagging doubts about God that you've never openly admitted. Deep down there is a growing sense of frustration. Maybe your life is so disconnected from your faith that you're acting more like a retired Christian than an active one.

Think back to when you first came to faith. Remember when you confessed your sin and asked for God's grace to cover you and carry you? Or do you recall the season in your life when you were the most fired up about God, when it seemed he touched everything around you and your passion for him was tangible? That same love is still available to fill you today, no matter how empty you may feel.

Thankfully, when we look to the Bible we see examples of others who played their own version of hunger games with

God. One guy was Nicodemus. He was known as *the* teacher of Israel and had worked his way up the religious ladder to its highest levels. His fame and reputation were known and people recognized him and celebrated him in the streets of the city.

You've likely heard of his meeting with Jesus. It was when talking to Nicodemus that Jesus dropped his famous quote in John 3:16 that "God so loved the world." Two things really strike me about Jesus' interaction with Nicodemus. One is the incredible risk that he took to meet with Jesus, which I never fully appreciated before. The other is that Nicodemus was already familiar with the idea of being born again, and Jesus completely reversed it and blew it up. He offered him a different kind of spiritual food than all his religious good deeds could acquire for him.

The sheer risk Nicodemus took to see Jesus is hard for us to grasp today. Nicodemus was a Jew and a Pharisee, a leader in the religious party of the middle class. They adhered to the letter of the law in an extreme fashion and focused on righteousness and faithfulness to God. Though Jesus reserved some of his harshest words for them, they were a dedicated group of believers seeking to please God.

Nicodemus also served on the Sanhedrin, the Jewish ruling council. This was an elite council of elders, chief priests, and teachers of the law, sort of like the United Nations for Jewish believers in Israel at that time (see Luke 22:66).

Nicodemus possessed clout and power. He knew the Old Testament inside and out and had committed much of it to memory, if not all of it. He oversaw the spiritual development of others, and dedicated himself to seeking God full-time. Wealth and influence were his, along with fame.

Rather than trying to trick Jesus with questions in broad daylight, as other Pharisees had done, he approached him alone, at night. His visit suggests a personal quest, an honest inquiry into Jesus' identity. Consider how radical this would have felt for Nicodemus. As the teacher of Israel he approached an unlearned, untrained Galilean and inquired about the most important aspect of Jewish teaching.

According to John 2, at this point Jesus had already gone through the temple overturning tables and casting out money changers. His actions had roused the fury of the religious leaders. If others on the ruling council learned of Nicodemus' visit, they might accuse him of following Jesus. He knew the risk; he had everything to lose. When Nicodemus went to meet with Jesus privately he was already moving outside of the realm of convention. He was taking a risk of faith that could have profound implications.

For these reasons, he goes to meet him after dark. Perhaps Jesus was staying in a guest chamber on top of someone's house. Nicodemus would have walked the quiet night streets and taken the outside staircase to the room, bypassing entering the house and being seen.[1] I envision the room, dimly lit by candlelight, as Nicodemus approached.

He addressed Jesus with respect as "Rabbi," meaning "great one," and placed himself as a learner by acknowledging Jesus as a great teacher. He implied there were others who desired to know more of Jesus. But Jesus did not thank Nicodemus for this incredible compliment from Israel's all-star teacher. He showed neither awe nor disdain toward Nicodemus for having sought him out, and he immediately turned to his need, peered into his heart, and offered fulfillment for his spiritual hunger.

The Games We Play

When we were kids my older brother would always destroy me at Monopoly, which is why I'm not really into board games or game shows today. However, my wife and her extended family love them. When my relatives come into town they turn on the Game Show Network, which airs old reruns of game shows. We sit around watching all these people in their '70s clothes playing *The Newlywed Game* and everyone in my family is glued to the screen, laughing along. The best part for me is hearing the contestants use phrases like "far out" and "can you dig it," while looking like they walked right off the set of *Saturday Night Fever.*

Nicodemus was a master at the religious game. I'm not suggesting his faith was anything less than devout or sincere, but it is hard to imagine anybody rising to the top of the religious food chain in ancient Israel without some smooth people skills and adept maneuvering. He knew how to work certain compromises and strike helpful deals. He excelled at the art of religious showmanship.

It is easy to let God into your life and then become adept at religion, at "playing the game." You know how to shift gears when you're talking to someone and find out they are a Christian. You can drop the right Christian phrases and play the part. You act one way at church and a completely different way at work, or on the basketball court, or standing in the kitchen. You believe all that stuff about Jesus, but you just don't see it playing out in your real life. But rather than admit this and begin to deal with it, you just get better at appearances.

Maybe your life or marriage looks more like the game Angry Birds than anything resembling Christianity. You've become distracted by a growing resentment toward people or organizations that have hurt you, so you hurl words and accusations at others. Or maybe your relationship with God feels like a big, confusing jumble of letters you can't make sense of, like the game Words With Friends.

Jesus is offering you something radical and profound, a life that fills you with meaning and purpose, but to access this life you must take the risk of being honest about where you are spiritually. In my life I had to come to the place where I could admit I'd been playing games with God. I had grown too comfortable and predictable. I had exchanged the life God called me to for one of mediocrity and comfort.

Is there a risk in your life that you feel God is leading you to take? Are you willing to go "all in" with God again? Will you step out in faith and re-transfer ownership of your life, money, relationships, career, and health? Nicodemus took a huge risk to visit Jesus, but without risk you miss the reward. In fact, playing it safe with Jesus is the riskiest thing of all.

Wake the Dead

Another surprising thing to me about Jesus' interaction with Nicodemus is how he flipped his understanding of new birth upside down. Jesus says: "I tell you the truth, no one can see the kingdom of God unless he is born again" (John 3:3). He referred Nicodemus to the maternity ward. "Born again" literally means "born from above."

The phrase "born again" brings all kinds of pictures to people's minds. It could recall everything from a co-worker to a Billy Graham crusade to Tim Tebow to the baffling behavior of Westboro Baptist Church members holding "God Hates Fags" signs. The phrase gets lost in all the talk of political campaigning and the voting block of the "born again." Everything from companies to sports franchises to restaurant chains are described as "born again" when they rebound. To recapture its real meaning, we need to revisit Jesus' use of the term.

The idea wasn't new to Nicodemus. According to scholar Alfred Edersheim, Jesus turned the tables on Nicodemus' understanding of this concept. The term "new birth" was used in different contexts; religiously it meant the change that came *after* one began to obey and as a *result* of one's obedience. Nicodemus would have thought the "second birth was the *consequence* of having taken upon oneself 'the kingdom;' not, as Jesus put it, the *cause* and condition of it."[2]

Nicodemus understood that Jesus meant something entirely different and radical when he used the term "new birth," as his response indicates. He asks, "How can a man be born when he is old?" (John 3:4). He knows the question is absurd. Of course one cannot re-enter the womb. He's the great teacher of Israel, but he's playing along with Jesus and thinking in natural terms.

Jesus was speaking about a spiritual resuscitation of our lives orchestrated by God. When we believe in Jesus, when we look to him, the miraculous occurs. New birth doesn't come *after* life change, but *before*. This supernatural event begins the process of living a new life under God.

Think about the miracle of childbirth. Before the birth of our first daughter, my wife Lori loved watching TLC's program *A Baby Story*. The reality-style program chronicled different couples' journeys from pregnancy through childbirth. I walked in once while she was watching the show only to hear a woman screaming in labor. For reasons I am sure you can understand, I did not want to hear someone giving birth in my living room. So we had some good-natured "TV wars" during her pregnancy. Soon enough, like the couples I saw on *A Baby Story*, our turn came for birthing classes. New dads who had already taken the same classes always asked me, "Have you seen the video?"

"No, what video?" I'd reply.

They would laugh and walk off, leaving me curious and a bit perturbed. Then midway through our birthing classes we watched "the video." It was something I really wasn't prepared for.

A brave lady gave birth on camera.

Watching it all unfold was shocking. These weren't tasteful camera shots, and there was zero editing. I kept thinking of my dad, who never even left the waiting room when my mom delivered. Here I was watching a graphic video to prepare me for the real thing.

"Are you okay?" my wife asked as she held my hand. (Shouldn't I be doing that for her?) I felt queasy. That video was more information than I needed at the moment. I worried about being in the room when my wife delivered. As someone averse to the sight of blood, who can't even handle any of the medical shows on TV, I feared I might pass out.

The day finally arrived. It was an icy January morning when we checked into the hospital at a bright and early 5:30 a.m. to induce labor. Over the next sixteen hours, family and friends piled into the waiting room, eating burgers and occupying every chair and every square inch of available floor space. At 10:18 p.m., Lori delivered. The doctor passed me scissors to cut the umbilical cord and, with trembling hands, I blindly obeyed. I felt overjoyed. The entire event was miraculous. Amazing. I stood in awe at the complexity of how God could accomplish the creation of a life. The beautiful cries of a newborn entering a world of colors, smells, shapes, and temperature adjustments filled the room.

In a parallel way being born again spiritually opens up a whole new world, the world of the spirit, and it is the beginning of a journey that involves an entire shift in worldview. Being born again implies that we were spiritually dead before coming to faith. We need more than mild-mannered self-improvement or pull-yourself-up-by-your-bootstraps common sense. We need more than a quick pep talk by the latest version of Dr. Phil. We're *dead*. Defibrillators won't help. No amount of chest compressions or mouth-to-mouth resuscitation will help. We're way past CPR.

In high school I had a job at a local hospital working in the copy room. Oddly, it was located in the basement right next to the morgue. I'd always see the employees of this area in white coats pushing stretchers into the room. They were around death all the time and would often crack jokes about it. They lost touch with how bizarre that sounded and felt to those of us who weren't familiar with seeing corpses.

This is the image that the Bible gives of us when it says we were "dead in [our] transgressions" (Eph. 2:5). We're lying on a stretcher with a white sheet pulled over us. We are unresponsive to all that God is and to all that he wants to do in our life.

Jesus literally came to bring us back from the dead. When we place our faith and trust in him we are going through our own resurrection; we are born again. Like a newborn infant we are now called to grow and mature as people of faith. It may begin for us when we pray a prayer for salvation or walk down the aisle at church, but there is so much more to being born again than that moment.

New Life, Not Just Improved Life

Bestselling author Anne Lamott chronicles her experience of becoming a Christian in *Traveling Mercies*. She writes of being asked on a plane, "Are you born again?" She thought for a moment and replied,

> Yes, I am. I believe that when you get on a plane, if you start lying you are totally doomed. So I told the truth: that I am a believer, a convert. I'm probably about three months from

slapping an aluminum Jesus-fish on the back of my car, although I first want to see if the application or stick-um in any way interferes with my lease agreement. And believe me, all this boggles even *my* mind. But it's true. I could go to a gathering of foot-washing Baptists and, except for my dreadlocks, fit right in. I would wash their feet; I would let them wash mine.[3]

The change that occurs in one's life after being born again should be surprising. And yet when we look at statistics, we see that most Christians live just like the rest of the culture. The Barna Group revealed the disturbing results from surveys they did on born-again believers. They found that:

- One-third of all adults (34 percent) believe that moral truth is absolute and unaffected by the circumstances. Slightly less than half of born-again adults (46 percent) believe in absolute moral truth.
- Only one-quarter of all adults (28 percent) believe that it is impossible for someone to earn their way into heaven through good behavior. Not quite half of all born-again Christians (47 percent) strongly reject the notion of earning salvation through their deeds.
- A minority of American adults (40 percent) are persuaded that Jesus Christ lived a sinless life while he was on earth. Slightly less than two-thirds of the born-again segment (62 percent) strongly believes that he was sinless.[4]

I find it shocking to read that over half of those who describe themselves as "born again" don't believe in moral absolutes or salvation through the free grace of God, and over one-third don't believe in the sinless life of Jesus. George Barna goes on to say that "although most Americans consider themselves to be Christian and say they know the content of the Bible, less than one out of ten Americans demonstrate such knowledge through their actions."⁵ Is it any wonder that we feel empty spiritually? These stats reveal that a significant portion of modern-day Christianity seems to be little more than lip service.

Being born again is about more than *assertion* of supernatural belief in Jesus; it is about *experiencing* this supernatural transformation that begins with faith. We can't make ourselves rise from the dead. God does this miraculously when we place our trust in Jesus. And he will continue to renovate us as we follow him in faith. He isn't trying to just give us a *better life*; he's offering a *supernatural new life* based on a new birth. The point of new birth is new life lived between forgiveness and eternity. Jesus came to bring abundant life to the religious and the irreligious, to the legalists and the lawless. He came to offer a new way of doing life. He desires we live through his power, aware of his control each moment.

Dallas Willard writes,

> To be born from above, in New Testament language, means to be interactively joined with a dynamic, unseen system of divine reality in the midst of which all humanity moves about—whether it knows it or not. And that, of course, is "The Kingdom Among Us."⁶

Being born from above indicates we are conscious of God's presence all around us. It is not that God is "up there" and we are "down here," hoping to get his attention. Throughout Scripture God's presence is indicated to be everywhere. In this new reality we "live and move and have our being" in God (Acts 17:28).

Through new birth we enter the kingdom of heaven. Often the term "heaven" in Scripture implies a space not only above us, but around us. God may be above us in his power and holiness, but he is also present around us in the nitty-gritty details of life, in our financial situation and our marriage difficulty. His domain, the heavens, includes dirty dishes, dirty diapers, and Monday mornings.

Too often we associate new birth with something we affirm intellectually. We have churches full of people who believe the right things about Jesus but are not passionate about any of them. Blaise Pascal once wrote, "God desires to move the will rather than the mind."[7] The real issue is more than what a person thinks, but what they are willing to live and die for, what they are passionate about, what moves their *will*.

God longs to take you from the maternity ward to the school of faith. He longs for you to go from the crib to walking, running, and leading in faith. He desires for you to forgive more completely, to give more generously, to trust more freely, and to experience his love more profoundly next year than this year. He doesn't simply want to change your mind; he wants to radically change your heart.

Alive to God

How do we bridge the gap between what we believe intellectually and what we experience practically? How do we experience more of the fulfilling love of God?

Jesus gives us insight when he says to Nicodemus, "I tell you the truth, no one can enter the kingdom of God unless he is born of water and the Spirit" (John 3:5). Some question whether or not water means baptism in this passage, and you can build a strong argument either way. Yet many early church fathers interpreted "water" in Jesus' statement to point to baptism.

When Paul wanted to challenge Christians to live out their faith and deal with sin in their lives, he reminded them of their baptism: "Since we have died to sin, how can we continue to live in it? Or have you forgotten that when we were joined with Christ Jesus in baptism, we joined him in his death?" (Rom. 6:2–3 NLT).

Can you remember your baptism? Maybe it was in a church or at a summer church camp. Perhaps it was with a small group around a swimming pool or in a creek or pond. Think back to that moment and what it stands for. Your baptism is a picture of what God has done in your life. According to the Bible, water baptism pictures how God incorporates people:

Into the name of the Father and of the Son and of the Holy Spirit (Matt. 28:19)

Into the forgiveness of your sins (Acts 2:38)

Into Christ Jesus (Rom. 6:3)

Into Jesus' death (Rom. 6:3)

Into one body (1 Cor. 12:13)

Your baptism represented an unmistakable burial and resurrection in Christ. William Willimon said, "In baptism we are initiated, crowned, chosen, embraced, washed, adopted, gifted, reborn, killed, and thereby sent forth and redeemed. We are identified as one of God's own, then assigned our place and our job within the kingdom of God."[8]

Some of my most special moments have centered on baptism. I remember my own baptism and how important it was to me. I've been privileged to baptize dear friends and family, and while living in Las Vegas I've even baptized Elvis (an impersonator of course). Baptism speaks to the reality of the victory of Jesus over the sin in our life.

Remember what your baptism was like and what it represents. Remember that you have been forgiven. Remember that you are God's! Remember you've been sent forth to live a new life "in Christ." Living this new life involves remembering our new identity that God has given us, as represented in baptism.

Jesus teaches that the new birth also involves the Holy Spirit. Placing our faith in Jesus, we receive the gift of the Spirit so that our essential reality is life in the Spirit. Paul calls the Holy Spirit the "Spirit of sonship" and claims that everyone who has the Spirit is a son of God (see Rom. 8:15). The Spirit's role is to make Christ known in our lives and transform us to be like Christ.

Part of the way we bring what we say and what we experience together is by being "filled with the Spirit" (Eph. 5:18). That Scripture could read, "allow the Holy Spirit to keep on filling you." There are a couple of implications here. One, our responsibility is not to fill ourselves, but to yield to God and allow him to fill us. Two, we are not passive. Just as we don't get drunk without drinking, we are not filled with the Spirit without yielding to the Spirit and inviting him to work in our life.

When I struggle with my experience of God, it is often because I have slowly drifted and ceased to consciously be filled with the Spirit. I allowed sin, habits, and the daily grind to press God from my thoughts, and I have become empty. Or, at other times, I have allowed religion to squeeze out a living relationship with Jesus. I did all the religious things, but without the right heart. Just as new birth is a work of the Spirit, renewal is also a work of the Spirit.

My first steps to recapture passion and love for Jesus involve inviting the Spirit to fill my life each day, each moment, and yielding to the Spirit's will. I begin in the morning with a few seconds in prayer: "God, I yield to you. Fill me with your Spirit today. This is your day." In this prayer I'm declaring my desire to live on his agenda and I'm opening myself up to his work.

You don't have to fight and claw through life on your own. Through surrender you can find yourself filled and empowered to live in Jesus' victory. The Christian faith isn't fundamentally about trying harder, but about opening one's hands and heart, putting up the white flag and admitting we were foolish to try and tackle our life and sin on our own. New birth by water and Spirit are the solution to our spiritual longing.

Indescribable Gift

A few years ago I read a story about teenage pregnancies. Some Los Angeles reporters discovered that girls in the inner city as young as thirteen had become pregnant . . . *intentionally*. When asked why they would have children so young, one girl said, "I just wanted someone to love. Is that so hard to understand?" Imagine the amount of heartache and the loneliness that could push a young teenage girl to pregnancy as a way to find love. Yet in our own way we are all looking for love—and often in the wrong places.

Nicodemus sought God's love based on his religious achievements. As a Pharisee he would have focused on external rules to attain righteousness—to the extreme. For instance, God commanded the people to rest on Saturday, the Sabbath. The Pharisees had a list of thirty-nine "forbidden works" on the Sabbath to ensure they did not accidentally work. Many of these rules had their own subcategories. They could not pull one hair from their beards or heads. They could not cut their fingernails. And on and on. This was just for the Sabbath day; they developed hundreds of other similar laws.

It would not be a stretch for Nicodemus to define himself by his track record.

Jesus described God's love to Nicodemus in some of his most popular words, which get lost in their familiarity. We've seen them held up in the crowd at football games and quoted on billboards. We get desensitized to them and miss the miracle God provided. We simply take his love for granted.

Try to suspend the familiarity and read this passage out loud, inserting your name: "For God so loved _____ that he gave his one and only Son, that whoever believes in him shall not perish but have eternal life. For God did not send his Son into the world to condemn _____ but to save _____ through him" (John 3:16–17).

Did you read it out loud? Was it awkward to insert your name? Did you hesitate to say it? Do you feel uncomfortable getting that personal with something God did for the world? After all, you're just one person among billions—and yet the world includes *you*! Don't miss the wonder of it! Resist the tendency to water this down or diminish its impact.

God doesn't just love you, he *likes* you. He likes you so much he would give up that which is most dear to him, his son, so that you could be in a relationship with him! Paul calls Jesus' sacrifice on the cross an "indescribable gift" (2 Cor. 9:15); has it become too describable for you? Are you still in awe of what it stands for? Are you still blown away by what it means?

Nicodemus was never quite the same after that encounter with Jesus. After the candles were blown out that night and the city slept, I imagine he thought long and hard about Jesus' statement, "For God so loved the world . . . "

After this encounter Nicodemus disappears from the record of Jesus' life, except for one brief moment when he stood up for Jesus at a religious meeting. Then we come to the end of

John's Gospel and find that along with Joseph of Arimathea, a man named Nicodemus took Jesus' body down from the cross. He "brought a mixture of myrrh and aloes, about seventy-five pounds. Taking Jesus' body, the two of them wrapped it, with the spices, in strips of linen. This was in accordance with Jewish burial customs" (John 19:39–40).

Nicodemus placed the body of Christ in a tomb. I assume he revisited that tomb many times, not to mourn but to marvel. He didn't have to play hunger games anymore. For Christ had risen, not only from the grave, but in his own heart as well.

QUESTIONS FOR DISCUSSION

1. On a scale of 1–10, where would you place your acceptance of God's love?

1   10

(struggle to accept God's love)   (fully accept God's love)

2. In what ways can God's indescribable gift of grace in Jesus become too describable?
3. What is the difference between loving someone and liking someone? What are the implications of God loving *and* liking you?
4. Discuss the thought that some Christians believe all the right things but are not passionate about any of them.
5. Jesus told Nicodemus that new birth was through water and spirit. Discuss the meaning of *water* and *spirit* and share your experience.
6. Brainstorm how you and your church can share Jesus' love with others.

2

all the lonely people

When I was 18, I was driving around at two in the morning, completely crying and alone and scared. I drove by this magazine stand that had this *Rolling Stone* that I was on the cover of, and it said, "Winona Ryder: The Luckiest Girl in the World." And there I was feeling more alone than I ever had.[1]

Winona Ryder

Remember where you were on 9/11?

I was in my office at the church I served in Southern California. My friend Carl stuck his head in and said I better come see something on TV. We gathered around a small TV in the center office area and watched in disbelief as the twin towers of the World Trade Center collapsed.

Words can't really describe the shock, disbelief, and grief we felt. I immediately called my wife and then my parents to tell them I loved them. And I thought about and prayed for the thousands who no longer had spouses, moms, or dads after that horrible day. Now, that event was over ten years ago, and we're all still shaken by it.

For me the most powerful and tragic footage I've seen of 9/11 is the film by the French brothers simply titled *9/11*. They were shooting a documentary on a firefighter near the towers when the attacks happened, and they captured raw footage of many of those heroes that day, including the only video that we have from inside one tower as the other collapsed.

I'll never forget watching the firemen inside the towers and hearing the huge crashing sounds that periodically came from outside. Suddenly I realized the sounds were the bodies of people hitting the ground, people who had jumped to their deaths. Totally. Unbelievable.

I found the documentary very moving; it brought me to tears many times. After watching it on television I didn't think I'd ever watch it again. It was simply too hard to digest. However, when the ten-year anniversary of 9/11 came around I decided I wanted to see it again and remember, so I purchased it. I don't want to ever forget those heroes that day and the sacrifices they made to help so many.

As I reflected on 9/11 during its ten-year anniversary I was reminded of how challenging that season was for our nation and for me. The tragic events of 9/11 happened within a month of my family and I moving from Texas to Southern California, where I took a new role on staff at a church. That tragic night of 9/11, I remember standing on the steps of the church as thousands of people packed into the auditorium to remember and mourn and pray. We were Americans. We were together. We did not stand alone.

And I had *never* felt so alone in my life.

The Word That Clears the Room

Moving to a new place only weeks before and leaving friends and connections exaggerated my sense of isolation after 9/11. I not only felt incredibly lonely, I felt guilty for feeling lonely. After all, there were so many who had lost loved ones, there was a mountain of rubble to clean up in New York City, the Pentagon had to be repaired, and the new war on terror was gearing up. Who was I to mope around?

All of this led me to bury my feelings, which in turn allowed them to fester and grow. I didn't realize that my wife was facing similar things that would lead her into a long season of depression. We both just buried everything going on inside of us, and I threw myself into my work.

Loneliness is a strong word conjuring strong emotion. We readily admit to being tired or weary, even hurt, but not to being lonely. The term strikes a chord deep within us that carries embarrassment. It is just uncool. In Douglas Coupland's novel *Miss Wyoming*, one character admits, "Loneliness and the open discussion of loneliness is the most taboo subject in the world. Forget sex or politics or religion. Or even failure. Loneliness is what clears a room."[2]

But loneliness is real, pervasive, and universal. We see it everywhere, from teenage suicide attempts to dating websites. Loneliness is not simply being alone, but being unfulfilled relationally, spiritually, and emotionally. It is a kind of emotional estrangement, a sense of being cut off or disconnected. We can feel lonely sitting in a crowded bus, a mall, a football stadium, or in the middle of a full church auditorium.

Loneliness touches us all. If you are a leader, you carry burdens no one else does, and you understand the weight of isolated responsibility. As the saying goes, "It's lonely at the top." Or perhaps you've joined the thousands each year who move. The moving van has carried your earthly possessions to a new location, but there is so much you've left behind. As the weeks turn into months, the feeling of loneliness grows, and you're frustrated at how difficult it is to make new friends. Or maybe high school graduation has finally occurred for your youngest child. The joy of such an achievement may feel satisfying—but the empty nest, not so much.

There are many unhealthy ways to deal with loneliness, and I think I've tried most of them. You can turn to unhealthy relationships, withdraw from the world, or retreat into the bottle or the party scene. I found that addiction can begin in an attempt to escape loneliness, but before too long it actually fosters it. The more you rely on a substance or a behavior, the more private your addiction becomes, the more secretive your actions become, the more *alone* you are. Work and hobbies offer nice diversions, but the end result of loneliness remains the same.

As you'd expect, loneliness has tremendous effects on the body. Studies have shown that it raises blood pressure, diminishes sleep, and puts one at risk of heart trouble. Dr. John Cacioppo of the University of Chicago said the damaging effects of loneliness are comparable to "obesity, sedentary lifestyles and possibly even smoking."[3]

So how do we face this issue? Shouldn't we no longer be lonely after coming to faith? Where is God in all of this?

It is important to distinguish between different experiences of loneliness. There is a loneliness that can only be fulfilled by other people. When God created Adam he said, "It is not good that man should be alone," so he formed a woman from Adam's side (see Gen. 2:18–22). Obviously this applies to marriage, but it also speaks to friendship in general. God's the one who said that isolation isn't good, and he created other people to meet our hard-wired need for companionship. This is why years of social research show that the best predictor of happiness is the quality of our social network and relationships with others.

Yet other people are not enough in themselves. Another dimension of loneliness can only be filled by God; he created the "God-shaped" void in our lives and only he can fill it. We can bandage this loneliness with a lot of things, but our relationship with God is the only thing that can really heal it.

The tricky thing with loneliness is that even with good friends and a loving God, we still experience it. You don't have to move to feel homesick and cut off from a joy you once knew. During certain seasons we just feel lonely for no particular reason, and it is hard to know what to do. I'm convinced the reality is that there is an experience of loneliness that remains in this fallen world and will only be healed in heaven. You can be the most spiritual person on earth and still experience loneliness. Read virtually any biography of a great person of faith, and you'll see this again and again.

Henri Nouwen, a brilliant Christian professor and author, wrote:

> Our life is a short time in expectation, a time in which sadness and joy kiss each other at every moment. . . . In every satisfaction, there is an awareness of limitations. In every success, there is the fear of jealousy. Behind every smile, there is a tear. In every embrace, there is loneliness. . . . And in all forms of light, there is the knowledge of surrounding darkness. . . . But this intimate experience in which every bit of life is touched by a bit of death can point us beyond the limits of our existence. It can do so by making us look forward in expectation to the day when our hearts will be filled with perfect joy, a joy that no one shall take away from us.[4]

Nouwen speaks of a loneliness that will remain until we experience the love, joy, and peace of heaven. In John 4, Jesus encountered a woman who experienced loneliness in multiple ways. In their conversation, Jesus offered comfort. This is my favorite encounter with Jesus in the Bible. I guess it is because I live in Las Vegas; I see this woman as representative of so many who live here and who long for *more*. Where Nicodemus was a spiritual leader, this woman was a spiritual outcast. Nicodemus strived for righteousness full-time; she had a long list of mistakes. But they both yearned for answers and companionship, and seeing how Jesus dealt with them both can help us in our own struggle.

The Thirst for Love

Jesus arrived at Jacob's well with his disciples around noon. Jacob's well sat about a quarter mile outside of Sychar, which was located about thirty miles north of Jerusalem. Because Jacob's well still exists, it is the only place where we absolutely know Jesus stood within a six-foot radius.[5] Jesus arrived at the well tired and hungry, and while his disciples were in town buying food, he encountered a Samaritan woman.

Women normally retrieved water in the morning and evening, when the temperature was cooler. What was this woman doing at the well at noon—alone? Probably avoiding those who went in the morning and evening. The well served as a gathering place. The women would walk in groups and share in conversation. A similar contemporary gathering place might be a coffee shop or a break room.

Jesus, being compassionate and caring, addressed her: "Will you give me a drink?" (John 4:7). This was unheard of; men did not openly talk with women in their culture and, as John says, "Jews do not associate with Samaritans" (v. 9). The term *associate* here means "use together with," and often referred to vessels. Jews did not drink out of the same vessels as Samaritans.[6]

The Samaritan woman was aghast at Jesus' request. To offer or receive water served as a contract in the ancient world. Such an act was an agreement to be friends. She responded, in essence, "Why do you, a Jew, want to be my friend?"[7]

Jesus crossed racial, ethnic, and religious barriers to connect with her in the experience of loneliness. This poor woman was rejected for being born a Samaritan and a woman. Being Samaritan, she was viewed by the Jews as an ethnic half-breed, not a full-blooded Jew. Nothing devastates like rejection for being who one is. Racial, ethnic, and social rejection leave scars that can remain through one's entire life. Jesus reached out to this Samaritan woman and tapped into her thirst for love and companionship. In the conversation that follows, we learn more about this woman's situation. Jesus said, "Go, call your husband and come back."

"I have no husband," she replied.

Jesus said to her, "You are right when you say you have no husband. The fact is, you have had five husbands, and the man you now have is not your husband. What you have just said is quite true" (see vv. 16–18).

Her jaw surely dropped. How could he know about her previous husbands? Why did he speak with such calm assurance? Could he really understand her pain?

This woman had felt the devastating pain of divorce. She knew relational loneliness. Perhaps she had been abused in her relationships. Perhaps she believed she was justified in all five divorces. Maybe she felt there was no other way. Irrespective, loneliness would have been a major factor in her life.

Maybe you have recently gone through a divorce and you understand relational devastation. You remember the pain that was delivered with the divorce papers. Or perhaps you have been single for many years and you wonder if Mr. Right will ever come along. Pretty soon Mr. Could-Be-Worse looks okay. You are tempted to lower your standards and settle for someone, anyone, in your life.

Often we think a companion will fill all our needs. We focus time and energy on finding a companion and playing the game. One newspaper ad read: "One-In-A-Million: Beautiful, romantic, outgoing, optimistic, honest, comedic DWF loves home life, dancing, traveling, picnics. Seeking the one: sweet, thoughtful, honest man. No head games."[8]

No head games? What was "beautiful, romantic, outgoing, and optimistic"?

We need relationships and friends, but illusions of romance filling one's primary emotional, spiritual, and psychological needs are dangerous. Marriage does not guarantee a life without loneliness. Dr. John Cacioppo said, "Marriages can be intense sources of loneliness. Being alone is about choice, and loneliness deals with one's perception of a relationship."[9] Many marriages are places of isolation and distrust, but Jesus reminds us that we can look beyond ourselves for spiritual resources that can sustain us.

Other people can never ultimately quench the thirst of our souls. Jesus asked for a drink, but he desired to give the Samaritan woman water for her soul. He reached out to meet her thirst with his living water. He offered the only drink that would satisfy.

The Drink That Satisfies

Marketers constantly appeal to our thirst:

"Have a Coke and a smile."
"Do the Dew."
"Gatorade: The ultimate thirst quencher."

"Dr Pepper: You make the world taste better."
"Got milk?"

Jesus appeals to thirst as well, but he offered more than a marketing slogan to the woman at the well. He said,

> "Everyone who drinks this water will be thirsty again, but whoever drinks the water I give him will never thirst. Indeed, the water I give him will become in him a spring of water welling up to eternal life." The woman said to him, "Sir, give me this water so that I won't get thirsty and have to keep coming here to draw water." (John 4:13–15)

The woman at the well initially missed the point. She got excited because she wouldn't have to make the ten-minute trek to the well every day. But Jesus is talking about quenching a spiritual thirst and meeting a spiritual need. He appeals to one of our most fundamental cravings by using the symbol of water.

Water constitutes the major element of all living matter; 50 to 90 percent of all living organisms' weight is water. In liquid and solid form, water covers 70 percent of the earth's surface. It comprises 78 percent of the human brain, 92 percent of blood plasma, and 80 percent of muscle tissue. Statistically, we die without water. "It takes less than a 1 percent deficiency in our body's water to make us thirsty. A 5 percent deficit causes a slight fever. An 8 percent shortage causes the glands to stop producing saliva and the skin to turn blue. A person cannot walk with a 10 percent deficiency, and a 12 percent deficiency brings death."[10] And just as we die physically without water, we die spiritually without Jesus.

In Jesus' day, everyone in Israel depended on rainfall to provide water. They lived in constant threat of drought. The Jordan River flowed, but it was inaccessible from many regions.

People stored water in springs, wells, cisterns, and pools. Because stagnant water became stale and even toxic over time, they understood the value of running water brimming with refreshment. Jesus offers himself as the lone fountain where we drink of the Spirit.

How can we experience living water when we are lonely? As Jesus conversed with the woman at the well, they discussed the concept of worship. The Samaritans believed that God was to be worshiped on Mount Gerazim. Jesus declared that the true place of worship was Jerusalem, but he claimed the time had come when people can worship in spirit and truth. Worship is one of the most powerful antidotes to loneliness. Paul wrote that we are to

> be filled with the Spirit. Speak to one another with psalms, hymns and spiritual songs. Sing and make music in your heart to the Lord, always giving thanks to God the Father for everything, in the name of our Lord Jesus Christ. Submit to one another out of reverence for Christ. (Eph. 5:18–21)

Paul points to singing as a way of being filled with the Spirit. He speaks of "psalms, hymns and spiritual songs." As we lift our voices in praise to God, we are renewed and refreshed.

I remember one Thanksgiving in college that became a defining moment for me. All my roommates had gone home to be with family and I was alone on the dorm floor. I literally had Ramen noodles for lunch and then I watched the Cowboys, my team, lose. It was a horribly lame day. Everything was going wrong and I was moping around feeling sorry for myself. Everybody else feasted with family; I ate Ramen. Everybody else laughed and had fun; I was stuck with *me*.

Out of boredom more than anything else, I grabbed my acoustic guitar and started playing. Then I began to think about God, and my noodling led to a half-hour of really bad singing and playing of worship songs. Thankfully, no one was around but God, and I'm hanging on to the fact that the Bible tells us to sing without stipulating that the singing must be on key! By the time I was finished, everything about my day looked so much better.

I had been so focused on what I didn't have, and worship moved me to remember all that I did have. It shifted my focus to God and the great work he had done in my life. It brought me into conviction about my sin and led me into joy over God's forgiveness. Not only that, the rest of the afternoon I remained mindful of God, and through spending time in prayer I made a decision I'd been struggling with: to change colleges. This became a transitional moment for me that I could have missed in my self-absorption.

Worship has the power to put everything in perspective and to connect us with the living God. Worship turns from the loneliness within to the fullness of God. It is a refocusing of our attention from our needs to the needs of others. As we worship, we dwell on God and his riches rather than ourselves and our lack. We experience his healing love. He has all the resources we need.

Paul also speaks of having grateful hearts, "always giving thanks to God the Father for everything" (v. 20). Each day we can choose how we will approach life. We can see what we lack or we can focus on what we have and give thanks to God for his goodness. A thankful attitude is a strong antidote to loneliness.

Another way we deal with loneliness is by getting alone with God in regular intervals in our lives. I'm not talking about ten minutes in the morning, but taking a day, or a few days, to get alone with God. Solitude provides inner fulfillment, whereas loneliness seems like emptiness. In solitude we are intentionally alone in order to reconnect with God and with who we are. In solitude we become comfortable in our own skin. These moments have been huge for me and they have left me with a deep sense of fulfillment. My loneliness did not simply vanish, but it was somehow muted by the important time I was spending with God.

Henri Nouwen wrote,

> It is in solitude that we discover that being is more important than having, and that we are worth more than the result of our efforts. In solitude we discover that our life is not a possession to be defended, but a gift to be shared. It's there we recognize that the healing words we speak are not just our own, but are given to us; that the love we can express is part of a greater love; and that the new life we bring forth is not a property to cling to, but a gift to be received.[11]

As we've said, people are another of God's solutions for loneliness and we need them desperately. Dietrich Bonhoeffer said,

> Let those who cannot be alone beware of community. . . . Let those who are not in community beware of being alone. . . . Each by itself has profound pitfalls and perils. One who wants fellowship without solitude plunges into the void of words and feelings, and one who seeks solitude without fellowship perishes in the abyss of vanity, self-infatuation, and despair.[12]

Both solitude and community are essential in dealing with loneliness. Connecting with people seems like a no-brainer, but it is more and more challenging in our world. Despite all the internet's benefits, scientists claim evidence that suggests the web can foster the experience of loneliness. One woman said this: "I sit late at night with a few cups of coffee, a few cigarettes, and my friend the internet, a good friend. . . . I feel lonely, sometimes even sorry for myself, wondering about love and things of the heart, wishing to be hugged and instead, there's only my keyboard and emptiness."

We all have acquaintances and colleagues, but do you have any *friends*? I mean the kind of friends you can call in the middle of the night and they will drop everything, climb out of bed, and be there for you. You don't need many—in fact, you're probably doing well if you have one. Studies have shown that many men don't have a single friend in their life.

I've had to come to the realization that this is my responsibility. Nobody is going to do this for me. I have to be proactive and focus on being the kind of friend I want to have.

Paul reveals that one way to be filled with the Spirit involves submitting "to one another out of reverence for Christ" (Eph. 5:21). Community is an essential ingredient in being filled with the Spirit. Living a Christian life is not something you can do alone. Make a commitment to get involved with a community of believers; join a small group that focuses on Bible study or service projects. We all know we *should* do this, but we'll never experience the benefits until we actually take action.

Will you choose to remain in isolation, hanging on to your secrets, or will you make a commitment to be the kind of friend to someone that you'd love to have? More than likely this commitment will evolve into something meaningful and real. And with technology such as Skype you can stay connected to people anywhere in the world. You aren't limited to the neighborhood anymore.

Sharing the Love

I love the story Steve Sjogren shares about a Christmas Eve when the Vineyard Community Church of Cincinnati shared the love. Rather than offering a traditional church service, they delivered doughnuts and coffee to workers around the city—police officers, firefighters, grocery store clerks, restaurant employees, and others. They shared God's love by encouraging others.

The following week Steve, the senior pastor, received a phone call from a local psychiatrist. The psychiatrist told him that two of his patients, who did not know each other previously, had been in a restaurant on Christmas Eve where they joined a dozen or so other lonely people on a night when the rest of the world gathered with family and friends.

Several people from Vineyard Community Church came in with coffee and doughnuts for the workers. They also put money in the jukebox, selecting some Diana Ross tunes. Mingling with the customers, they eventually had the whole place dancing to the music. They helped them get their minds off the fact they were alone. The psychiatrist said, "I just want to thank you. Both my patients said they were experiencing the worst Christmas Eve of their life, but it wound up being the best Christmas Eve they ever had. Thank you for caring."

Then he said, "I have one final question: Do you play Diana Ross music in your church?"

Steve knew there was no good answer to that, so he said, "Not yet!"

When the woman at the well encountered Jesus, she was amazed. Her view of Jesus progressed from calling him a "Jew" (John 4:9) to "Sir" (v. 11) to "prophet" (v. 19). The more we learn of Jesus, the more amazed we are by him. Our problems appear smaller as he grows larger. The woman left her water jar, ran back to town, and said, "Come, see a man who told me everything I ever did. Could this be the Christ?" (v. 29). And many Samaritans came to believe because she shared the water.

Sharing the love of Christ with others is a strong counter to loneliness. As we serve and use our gifts, we have the thrill of being used by God. Jesus desires for us to see people and situations as opportunities for encouragement, as divine appointments where we share his love.

Who around you needs living water? Will you give them a drink? On the cross Jesus said, "I thirst." He thirsted so that we might thirst no more. His love is available in the down times when it feels like nobody is noticing and nobody cares. *He* notices, and he has demonstrated his care in countless ways. If he set a divine appointment to meet a five-time divorcée at a well, rather than a political power player or a celebrity, he's also ready and willing to make time for you.

QUESTIONS FOR DISCUSSION

1. How often do you experience loneliness in an average week?
2. What are some unhealthy ways people deal with loneliness?
3. Discuss the statement, "You can be the most spiritual person on earth and still experience loneliness."
4. What is the difference between solitude and loneliness?
5. How does one rehydrate, so to speak, and drink of Jesus' living water?
6. What are some practical ways you or your church can "share the water" with others?

3

hands in the cookie jar

Me not "take" cookies, me "eat" the cookies.

Cookie Monster

My wife makes amazing chocolate chip cookies. Sometimes I'll come home and the smell of them baking will be wafting through the house. One day I came home and there were cookies already made, sitting on a plate. The only problem was Lori ordered me not to eat the cookies. They were for my daughter's class the next morning and we didn't have enough dough to make more.

Hands off the cookies!

But a little later, Lori left the kitchen. I was watching the news and suddenly I began to think about the cookies. I could hear the cookies calling me. I began to rationalize: *I've had a long day, and after all, I need a cookie . . . or two.*

I bet she hasn't counted them. I deserve a cookie. I paid for the cookies! I bet if I just take one, she'll never know. It will be my little secret.

So I slipped into the kitchen and ate one. It was so awesome . . . still warm . . . the chocolate melted in my mouth. (Getting hungry yet?) Then I ate another. At this point I knew I should stop eating the cookies, but I figured one more wouldn't hurt. Plus, I was going to work out tomorrow, so I'd make it right!

I thought my secret was safe. I thought I could dip my hand in the cookie jar, so to speak, and no one would ever find out. Well, a few hours later I heard my name yelled from across the house: "Judson!" That was what my mom called me when I was in trouble as a kid. And it is amazing how our wives, without even knowing that, go there. I was busted for eating the cookies.

The conversation went something like this: "Jud, I told you not to eat these cookies. They are for Emma's school, and now there may not be enough. I'll have to go to the store, buy more dough, and make more. Why did you eat the cookies?"

I answered the way any two-year-old does when he or she gets in trouble: I looked down at the floor, shook my head from side to side, and said, "I don't know."

What I needed in that moment was grace, even though I didn't deserve it. What we all need is grace, because too often we keep secrets. Too often we put our hands in the cookie jars of life, where we know they shouldn't be.

And it doesn't take long for most of us to amass quite a guilt collection. We carry it around on our shoulders and allow it to weigh us down—lust, revenge, anger, words spoken, deeds done. Guilt comes in many shapes and sizes, but it always comes.

Have you put your hand in the cookie jar lately? Are you buried under the weight of guilt for something you desperately wish you could undo? Do you feel like you will never be enough, like you will never change? Even when you can't explain all your actions, you serve a God who took action on your behalf.

In John 8 we read about a woman who experienced her share of guilt. Her encounter with Jesus teaches us much about guilt, grace, and forgiveness.

Caught in the Act

The seven-day Feast of Tabernacles had been celebrated. People had come from all over Israel to rejoice in God's past and present provision. Jesus had shown up in Jerusalem about halfway through the feast.

On the eighth day of the feast, considered a Sabbath, Jesus sat in the temple courts teaching the people. The religious leaders dragged in a woman and angrily threw her before Jesus. "Teacher," they said to Jesus, "this woman was caught in the act of adultery. In the Law Moses commanded us to stone such women. Now what do you say?" (John 8:4–5).

Stone faces and stones in their hands. The woman must have been terrified and embarrassed. Within moments she found herself exposed and hurled onto death row. From secret delight to public humiliation. The accusation: guilty of adultery, punishable by death.

The scene appears fishy from the beginning. How does one "happen" to catch someone in the act of adultery? It takes two to tango; where was the man? He was equally guilty. Maybe he was paid off to set her up, or he could have been a friend of the religious leaders. One thing is clear—the religious leaders were using this question as a trap, in order to have a basis for accusing Jesus (see v. 6). Rather than offering the woman a helping hand, the religious leaders set her up. She had nowhere to run, nowhere to hide, and her guilt was real.

We often *feel* guilty because we *are* guilty. Today this is a revolutionary thought, as we view any guilt as a negative. It was Friedrich Nietzsche, probably the most influential philosopher of modern thought, who contended that good and evil are not realities but things derived from Christianity. His teaching still has great trickle-down influence on the way we view guilt today. Sigmund Freud praised Nietzsche for having a greater self-knowledge than any other human. Adolf Hitler was so fascinated by him that he personally presented his complete works to Benito Mussolini. Yet Nietzsche himself fought to bury his past and his faith.

Nietzsche's father and grandfather were both pastors, and for a while Nietzsche was a devout young person. Paul Deussen writes of their religious confirmation on Easter 1861:

> When the candidates for confirmation went in twos to the altar, where they knelt to receive their consecration, Nietzsche also knelt, and as his closest friend, I knelt with him. I remember well the sense of holiness and detachment from the world that filled us during the weeks before and after confirmation. We would have been quite prepared there and then to die in order to be with Christ, and all our thinking, feeling and activity was resplendent with a more earthly serenity—this of course was an artificially reared little plant, which could not endure very long.[1]

Eventually Nietzsche turned his back on his faith and took his stance against Christianity. He chose to bury his guilt and rationalize it away. In his book *Beyond Good and Evil*, he argued that since we are beyond these ancient ideas, most of our guilt is false guilt. Yet the Bible is clear that we experience guilt because God has created us to regret our wrongdoing. We bury it and ignore it at a high price to ourselves.

Nietzsche himself paid a high price. On January 3, 1889, upon seeing a man whip a horse on the Piazza Carlo Alberto in Turin, Italy, he had a complete mental and emotional breakdown. For the next ten years Nietzsche lingered in madness, a pathetic figure. Guilt alone did not lead to his breakdown, but it surely influenced it. All of us must learn to take our guilt to God, or like a cancer it will slowly devour us. The woman caught in adultery was truly guilty, but she was not beyond grace.

The Defense

Initially, Jesus did not respond to the religious leaders' accusation. He bent down and wrote on the ground with his finger. This is the only record of Jesus writing. People have speculated that he wrote the sins of the religious leaders gathered around. Some say he wrote Scripture. Maybe he just doodled! But as he knelt, the leaders kept questioning him; they planned to snare Jesus in a catch-22. If he sentenced the woman to death, the Roman government would intervene. They alone could legally demand an execution.

If Jesus condoned a stoning, he might lose popularity. The crowd had followed him and had been attracted to his compassion. But if he told the leaders to let her go, they would accuse him of violating the law of Moses.

The leaders believed Jesus was cornered, but Jesus rose to give one of the most profound statements in Scripture: "If any one of you is without sin, let him be the first to throw a stone at her" (John 8:7). Then Jesus knelt again and resumed writing on the ground.

Silence. A few awkward moments of anger turning to introspection. The rocks fell to the ground one at a time. The text says the older men dropped their rocks and walked away first. No doubt recalling a lifetime's worth of mistakes and failures, they were quick to leave. By moving the focus off the woman, Jesus forced them to see their own guilt.

Jesus' concern was not the woman's innocence, but that she be treated fairly. If she was to be judged, the witnesses were to come forth and be just and impartial (see Deut. 19:15–19). These religious leaders were neither! For somebody to throw a stone, he had to testify to eyewitness accounts. Jesus was not trying to throw out the process of law and legal procedure; he was exposing this trial as a sham!

The Verdict

Eventually everyone drifted off, leaving Jesus alone with this woman. He looked up at her and said, "'Woman, where are they? Has no one condemned you?' 'No one, sir,' she said. 'Then neither do I condemn you,' Jesus declared" (John 8:10–11).

Beautiful words from the lips of a Savior. *Neither do I condemn you.* Under Jewish law no one could be condemned by a single witness, and Jesus did not desire to condemn. He came not to condemn the world but to save the world (see John 3:17). He showed her pure, unmerited, undeserved grace.

We are quick to judge, but what accusations could be leveled at us? For Nicodemus it could have been pride; for the woman at the well and this woman at the temple, adultery. No one wants to be a public spectacle by having their sins paraded around. This woman received pardon and a second chance in the midst of her humiliation. And Jesus has shown that same grace to millions through the ages.

This scene gives us caution. Too often Christians and churches shoot their wounded. When people fail, they need to be restored with a heart of compassion. It is too easy to rail against people who don't have our particular sin struggle.

Blacklisted

My friend Barry McMurtrie tells a story about Allison, a young girl his family took under their wing. Allison came from a hopeless home life. Her mother bounced from one relationship to another, and Allison never knew whom her mother would be bringing home.

Yet on her own Allison discovered the church Barry pastored. Much of the church was made up of street kids, and in that special community she found a family at church. She met a young man from a Christian home who told her he loved her and would marry her. But when she became pregnant, the man said God told him to buy a motorcycle and ride across Australia.

Some time after Allison had her baby, the father came back and told her he was sorry. He claimed he had made a mistake and said he loved her, but when she became pregnant again, he left again.

What does one do? Some would say to throw her out of the church because you are not allowed more than one mistake! It is tragic that we have a black-and-white list of sins. On the white list there is gossip, and you can gossip your way to the highest leadership positions of the church. But if your sin is on the blacklist, you are out. Allison was on the blacklist now, with two kids outside of marriage.

One day at Barry's church a guest speaker began to verbally attack unmarried mothers. Allison had moved to another town, but had returned to visit that weekend. Barry's secretary came to Barry during the message and said, "Allison just went outside."

Barry got up and followed her outside. He said, "Here is a kid who has made a mess of her life, with her raincoat over her two little children, trying to protect them from the rain, and crying her eyes out. She looked at me with tears in her eyes and said, 'He made me feel so dirty.' I said, 'I know, but Jesus would never do that.'"

I'm ashamed to think of how often the church has just made people feel dirty. Of course, we all sin, and in this sense we are all dirty, but the message of the gospel is that we can be clean through faith in Christ. He came to wash the dirt away.

Allison returned home crushed by the pastor, but thankfully not by Jesus, whom she still follows. Our calling is to live like Jesus, to meet people where they are, to be approachable, and to share Jesus' healing.

Will we be characterized by grace or judgment? We are flawed and will never have a perfect estimation of another person in this life. We will err, so we should choose to err on the side of grace rather than judgment. When people make mistakes they need our love more than our wrath. They need our concern more than our criticism. They need our compassion more than our anger.

Stranded without Grace

Some time ago my car broke down while I was speaking at a retreat in a rural area. I brought it to a repair shop and borrowed a church member's van so Lori and I could drive to the city for a date. On the way, an officer pulled me over for speeding. When he asked if my driver's license was correct, I admitted that the address was wrong. When he asked for my insurance, I informed him I had borrowed the car. He raised his eyebrows.

Lori searched frantically through the glove box but could not find any insurance documents. The officer asked where the owners of the car lived. I could not remember exactly. I mentioned that I could drive him there if he had an hour.

He didn't smile.

Things were moving from bad to worse. Under normal circumstances, I never play the "I-am-a-poor-minister-just-trying-to-do-something-good-so-please-have-mercy-on-me" routine. But these weren't normal circumstances. For all he knew, I had stolen the car.

"Well, officer," I said, "I am so sorry. I am a pastor and was speaking at a retreat in the next town. My car broke down there, and we were stranded. We borrowed our friend's van so we could go to the city. Did I mention I am a *pastor*, and we were *stranded*?"

He glanced at Lori, who was still digging through the glove box, and then looked back at me. I offered the most pitiful face I could muster.

"You're a pastor?" he asked.

"Yes," I said, in my most pastoral voice.

Long pause.

"Slow it down and drive safely," he said, as he handed my license back. I breathed a huge sigh of relief. What I had just experienced was grace. I deserved a ticket; I received mercy. I deserved punishment; I received pardon.

The Bible says that for our sin we deserve death—plain and simple. But because of what God did through Jesus, we can be in a right relationship with him and we can be forgiven. Once we realize that we deserve death, everything takes on the form of grace. It is by grace that we live, work, and experience life. It is *all* grace.

The grace of God is only one source of healing for our guilt. Time alone will not suffice. C. S. Lewis said,

We have a strange illusion that mere time cancels sin. I have heard others, and I have heard myself, recounting cruelties and falsehoods committed in boyhood as if they were no concern of the present speaker's, and even with laughter. But mere time does nothing either to the fact or to the guilt of a sin. The guilt is washed out not by time but by repentance and the blood of Christ.[2]

Have you been carrying guilt around, thinking that more time will heal your past mistakes? You don't have to wait. Jesus offers full forgiveness that you can experience today.

Any time we talk about guilt, we should recognize that there is such a thing as false guilt. The Bible describes people who have a weak conscience (see 1 Cor. 8:7–12); they believe some things are sins that are not really sins. Such people may feel guilty because their house isn't always spotless or if they're not busy every minute.

On the other extreme, some people experience no guilt; they have what the Bible calls a seared conscience. A seared conscience is one that has been violated so many times it no longer feels guilt (see 1 Tim. 4:2). Timothy McVeigh, for instance, went to his death expressing no regret for killing many innocent men, women, and children in the Oklahoma City bombing; he said they were simply "collateral damage." We can sear our conscience so much that we no longer feel guilt. But this does not mean we aren't guilty. God determines whether we are guilty or not, regardless of feelings.

We don't have to live with a seared conscience or a weak conscience; we can have a clean conscience. In the book of Hebrews we read,

Therefore, brothers, since we have confidence to enter the Most Holy Place by the blood of Jesus . . . let us draw near to God with a sincere heart in full assurance of faith, having our hearts sprinkled to *cleanse us from a guilty conscience* and having our bodies washed with pure water. (10:19, 22, emphasis added)

God does not delight in our guilt. He desires that we bring our guilt to him and be cleansed. Jesus died once for all to make that possible. A story by Garrison Keillor illustrates this. He writes,

Larry the Sad Boy . . . was saved 12 times in the Lutheran church, an all-time record. Between 1953 and 1961 he threw himself weeping and contrite on God's throne of grace on 12 separate occasions and this in a Lutheran church that wasn't evangelical, had no altar call, no organist playing "Just As I Am without One Plea" while a choir hummed and a guy with shiny hair took hold of your heartstrings and played you like a cheap guitar. This is the Lutheran church, not a bunch of hillbillies. These are Scandinavians, and they repent the same way that they sin: discreetly, tastefully, at the proper time. . . . Twelve times! Even we fundamentalists got tired of him. . . . God did not mean for us to feel guilt all our lives. There comes a point when you should dry your tears and join the building committee and start grappling with the problems of the church furnace and . . . make church coffee and be of use, but Larry kept on repenting and repenting.[3]

What are you carrying around in your backpack of guilt? What do you need to lay down? Maybe it's an affair that happened years ago. A broken marriage or a broken family may haunt you. Perhaps it's words that were spoken in anger that you would do anything to take back. Whatever it is, with God's grace, you can unlock those shackles and be free to live a new life. Let God forgive you. Allow him to unlock the prison bars of guilt and let you walk free.

After declaring grace for the woman caught in adultery, Jesus said, "Go now and leave your life of sin" (John 8:11). In essence he said, "You are set free. Go and live like it."

We often act as if we are forgiven and waiting for heaven. But grace and repentance go hand in hand. Grace is given freely, not to be abused but to motivate and empower change. The woman caught in adultery not only received that grace, she was challenged to live responsibly in it.

On the *Today* show, at the height of the Clinton sex scandal in the late '90s, Billy Graham talked with Katie Couric. He shared his view of Clinton's choices. In the end, he referred to Jesus' encounter with the woman caught in adultery and repeated Jesus' challenge: he who is without sin should cast the first stone. The next morning on the *Today* show, William Bennett presented the other side: go and sin no more. Both aspects are equally important. Both are part of being a follower of Jesus. But grace always comes before law; "neither do I condemn you" precedes "go and sin no more." Life change is the inevitable result of experiencing grace, not the other way around.

Dropping Our Rocks

In heaven there is much rejoicing when the lost are found, when they lay their guilt at God's feet and enter into his love. But on earth not everyone rejoices. Many, like the religious leaders with stones in their hands, have a hard time with grace. Consider the older brother in Jesus' parable of the lost son. You probably remember from the story that the younger brother took his inheritance and squandered it partying; he shamed his family and crushed his father.

When he returned home, the father ran out to greet him, put his arms around him, and threw a party for him. The older brother, dutifully working in the field, heard music and approached the house. He was angry when he learned that his brother had come home and his family was celebrating; he refused to join the festivities.

When the father learned his older son would not enter the party, he went out to talk to him. The older son calls his younger brother "this son of yours" and then implicates his father. Behind the words of this story lurks a deeper issue in the older brother—resentment. He says,

> Look! All these years I've been slaving for you and never disobeyed your orders. Yet you never gave me even a young goat so I could celebrate with my friends. But when this son of yours who has squandered your property with prostitutes comes home, you kill the fattened calf for him! (Luke 15:29–30)

Resentment is alive and well in the church today too. We longtime Christians may become bothered when attention rests on wayward people who come into a relationship with Christ, but God commands us to extend to them the same grace that he extends to us.

Another trait we see in the older brother is self-righteousness. In Luke 15 we find Jesus telling stories to defend himself against the religious leaders who were accusing him of hanging out with riffraff. He attacked their self-righteous attitude. In this instance, the older brother assumes the role of the Pharisee. After all, he did not squander away his life. He did not party until he dropped and woke up in the gutter of life. He had higher standards. Yet the older brother is just as lost and in need of grace as the wayward younger son. The difference is that the wayward son knew it because it was so apparent. The elder brother could not see his resentment and self-righteousness as sin. He represents a lostness that is extremely hard to break through.

Henri Nouwen wrote,

> Unlike a fairy tale, the parable provides no happy ending. Instead, it leaves us face to face with one of life's hardest spiritual choices: To trust or not to trust in God's all-forgiving love. I myself am the only one who can make that choice. In response to their complaint, "This man welcomes sinners and eats with them," Jesus confronted the Pharisees and scribes not only with the return of the prodigal son, but also with the resentful elder son. It must have come as a shock to these dutiful religious people. They finally had to face their own complaint and choose how they would respond to God's love for sinners.[4]

That is a choice each of us must make. We can quickly shift into a mode of determining who is and isn't acceptable to God. Self-righteousness and resentment creep into our lives. We miss the experience of God working in our lives to touch others. We miss the joy of seeing someone come into a relationship with Christ.

Neither do I condemn you. Go and sin no more. In one way or another, these words have been spoken to every Christian. Will we lay our guilt down? Will we reach out to the guilty and love them with open arms? Will we allow Jesus' words to become *our* words?

QUESTIONS FOR DISCUSSION

1. Discuss the difference between healthy and unhealthy guilt.
2. Why is it so difficult for many Christians to accept God's forgiveness?

3. On a scale of 1–10, where would you place your acceptance of God's forgiveness?

1   10

(struggle with accepting   (accept forgiveness
forgiveness)   freely)

4. Jesus said, "If any one of you is without sin, let him be the first to throw a stone at her" (John 8:7). What sins in others do you particularly want to throw stones at?

5. How do Christians act like the older brother in Jesus' parable of the prodigal son?

6. How can you or your church practically help people discover God's forgiveness?

4

riding the roller coaster

Life is all about timing . . . the unreachable becomes reach-
able, the unavailable become available, the unattainable . . .
attainable. Have the patience, wait it out. It's all about timing.

Stacey Charter

The Texas Giant stands over fourteen stories tall, tower-
ing above Six Flags Over Texas. It is one of the largest,
fastest wooden roller coasters in the world.

One scorching day I endured a two-and-a-half-hour wait
to maintain face with my wife. I pondered my strategy while
looking at the gigantic coaster. *Make sure the belt is secure,
take off your glasses, hold on tight, don't raise your hands
for any reason, lecture Lori about keeping her hands down,
grit your teeth, and pray it will be over soon.*

At last, we climbed into our seats. I took a deep breath and considered what lay before me: 4,920 feet of wood and materials crafted to thrill. I knew I could handle all the little dips and twists and turns; it's usually the big drop that gets me. My wife smiled and laughed, giddy at the thought of the ride. (I remind myself that thousands of people have done this. I am a man! Show no fear.)

The coaster began to climb. And climb. And climb. *This isn't so bad*, I thought, before looking down as we passed the top peak. Suddenly all of Texas lay before my eyes. Then we nose-dived for the ground. Somewhere in my mind lurked the thought that I paid for this, but in the moment it was too much. I gripped the railing with all my might. My stomach shot up into my throat. My muscles tensed. My heart stopped. My body jostled. And of course, my wife screamed for joy and lifted her hands!

When we finally came to a stop, I peeled my white knuckles off the bar and got out of the cart. A wooden roller coaster bounces you harder than a steel one. This one literally bounced me into la-la land. I slowly walked toward a bench and sat down to recover.

Life is a lot like a ride on a roller coaster: One minute everything is fine, and the next minute we're nose-diving out of control, jostled by the G-force of a long drop. One moment we feel secure, and the next devastating pain enters our lives. One moment we feel healthy, and the next we are on our back in a hospital bed staring at the ceiling. Perhaps it is a tragedy that comes without warning. Maybe it's a di- agnosis that redirects the future. Unfortunately, with life we can't just climb out of the seat and be through. Sometimes it keeps going no matter how damaged our heart is.

What kind of pain are you facing? Maybe it is chronic pain that only seems to get worse and consumes your every waking thought. It could be emotional pain from abuse suffered in childhood or marriage, or the more subtle variations you face at work or with family members. Perhaps it is spiritual pain toward God for letting you down in a way you perceive to be colossal.

We have seen Jesus offer spiritual fulfillment for our emptiness, companionship for our loneliness, and forgiveness for the weight of guilt. He also offers strength and peace in physical and emotional pain. Pain is something all of us wrestle with at varying levels. A Jewish proverb states, "Not to have had pain is not to have been human." The question is not whether we will suffer, but *when*.

Peace in Pain

Jan is one of the most joyous, well-loved people I know; she brings laughter and encouragement to everyone. But as we sat in her living room one spring day she expressed no joy, only sadness. We were planning her funeral.

Months before, she had been diagnosed with ALS, a mysterious disease without cure that paralyzes those who suffer from it. Jan had deteriorated rapidly, and she was already confined to a wheelchair. She had lost control of one arm and could hardly walk more than a few steps. She lived with a feeding tube. Some days she could not talk and for brief periods lost control of her breathing. She fully expected to simply stop breathing soon. That day in her living room our hearts were breaking, but we were not alone; Jesus' presence brought comfort.

Jan is no stranger to physical challenges and pain. As a child she suffered unmerciful physical abuse at the hands of alcoholic parents. Upon reaching adulthood the psychological, spiritual, and physical pain continued. Just as she was

71

about to deliver her first child, her husband of seven years brought divorce papers to the hospital; Jan was devastated as she delivered her daughter, who would be her beacon of hope through turbulent years.

After the delivery, doctors accidentally severed the femoral artery in Jan's right leg. They managed to save her leg, but severe pain plagued Jan the rest of her life. Vascular pain is some of the worst pain imaginable; Jan said her leg felt as if it had been dipped in acid. Between Jan's divorce and physical pain, her anger at God increased.

Jan married again, but her husband was unable to show affection and the marriage lasted one year. Anger and hate toward God and her first husband consumed everything. The only love that remained was toward her child. In these years she "fine-tuned" hate while tremendous physical pain pierced her right leg.

To cope, Jan partied. On New Year's Eve 1984, when she ran out of liquor, the obvious thing was to go to the local Safeway and get more. She walked in shortly before midnight and met Frank Frisbee, an old acquaintance. He realized she was drunk and sensed her brokenness. As they talked he said, "Jan, it's time you get your life together. You are going nowhere but down. You don't have to live like this."[1]

Jan was drunk and furious. After telling Frank off, she felt so shaken by the encounter she left the grocery store without purchasing anything. She says, "I walked into Safeway in 1984 and walked out in 1985, and my life would never be the same."[2]

Through a series of events Jan became a dedicated Christ-follower. She forgave key people and gradually let go of hate and anger. She also fell in love with and married Frank, whom she had run into in Safeway.

Jan wondered if she would be healed now that she was reaching out to God in faith. But after her conversion, her leg pain actually grew worse. Future years would involve more surgeries and threats of losing her leg. The pain was only bearable because of her faith in God. Jan says, "God knew I could not have tolerated the physical pain without his strength. Without God I would have died. I would have drugged myself to death. Physical pain is nothing compared to spiritual pain."[3]

Just when things were settling down, Jan began to lose control of one arm. Soon she had trouble holding her head up and doing the simplest things. Then came the wheelchair, the feeding tube, and finally the official diagnosis: ALS. Jan says, "Those days were sad, but not because of the pain. I was sad to leave my Frank alone. I asked God to have mercy on him."[4]

Jan's daughter moved home to help. People prayed for her healing. Jan began to take a strict regimen of vitamins, yet all to no avail.

I left Jan's house that spring morning feeling so helpless. Here was one of the most committed women I knew. Why was she suffering like this? Why wouldn't God heal her? Why did she have to carry so much pain? We braced ourselves for the phone call informing us that Jan had passed on.

The call never came.

That summer something miraculous happened. Jan regained strength in her neck. She began to hold her head up longer and she could swallow more easily. The doctors were shocked and could offer no explanation. Slowly, over the next several months, Jan had an amazing rebound; she began to experience recovery and was soon singing in the church choir again. She became active in her community and once again instilled love and joy in everyone she encountered.

Where the doctors have no answers, Frank and Jan have no doubt: God healed her. But even if he had taken her home, she was ready. She said,

73

People ask me regularly, "How can you smile?" I reply, "My pain has nothing to do with my smile; my smile has nothing to do with my pain. I have a Savior who loves me and died for me. As long as I have the Holy Spirit overflowing in me every day, physical pain is something I can get through."[5]

Today the doctors remain stunned and Jan remains active. She has endured more pain than most, but she has discovered healing in the midst of the pain. Her advice to those who are suffering is, "Don't look at your illness; look at the Lord. The only hope for anyone in pain is clinging to God. It is not just trust but totally clinging. He literally supersedes. He numbs the pain and comforts it better than any medicine or doctor. If you focus on the trial, your eyes will be off the cross. You will inevitably focus on yourself and your sorrow." That is good advice, because one day the roller coaster will dip, and we must deal with the pain inflicted.

Hurts So Good?

Pain is not all bad. In general, it serves a needed function in our lives. Without pain we would not be aware when we twist an ankle or injure a knee. The body has an amazing pain network. Pain serves as an alert or a warning that something is going on.

I was reminded of this at the gym one day. I have two rules of basic gym etiquette: (1) never make noise unless you are lifting a LOT of weight (have you ever heard someone grunting and groaning only to see they are barely lifting the bar?), and (2) never break your form. That day I got too macho and broke both rules.

Earlier that morning I aggravated my back while lifting. My body's pain network told me to call it a day, but I continued to lift. As I eked out my last curl, I broke form. Suddenly, a piercing pain shot up my back; I had pushed my muscles over the edge. I fell to the floor and tried not to yelp as I practically crawled to the locker room.

For a week I could hardly get out of bed. I reflected on how joyful I would be if my back just functioned properly. Never mind the fact that a few days earlier my back worked fine and I was not the happier for it.

Dr. Paul Brand said,

> The one legitimate complaint you can make against pain is that it cannot be switched off. It can rage out of control, as with a terminal cancer patient, even though its warning has been heard and there is no more that can be done to treat the cause of pain. But as a physician I'm sure that less than one percent of pain is in this category that we might call out of control. Ninety-nine percent of all the pains that people suffer are short-term pains: correctable situations that call for medication, rest, or a change in a person's lifestyle.[6]

We may concede that, in general terms, pain serves a healthy function. The problem is pain does not enter our lives "in general"; it enters specifically. In Jan's case, it was a debilitating disease. In your case, it may be in the form of a tragedy, loss of a loved one, a crippling accident, or child abuse.

Some pain is not good.

Love's Reach

Jesus met a woman in the crowd who suffered greatly. She understood the devastating effect of pain. She reached out to Jesus in her suffering and touched him in faith. Through her experience, we learn valuable lessons about faith, healing, and the love of God.

This woman sought Jesus while he traveled to heal Jairus' daughter. Jairus was a synagogue ruler whose twelve-year-old daughter had fallen deathly ill. Jairus threw himself at Jesus' feet and asked for a miracle. Jesus agreed, and while he made his way to heal her, this woman reached out, believing Jesus cared and could mend her life.

Where Jairus had clout, status, and power, this woman had nothing. Jairus is mentioned by name; this woman is anonymous. She "had been subject to bleeding for twelve years, but no one could heal her. She came up behind him and touched the edge of his cloak, and immediately her bleeding stopped. 'Who touched me?' Jesus asked" (Luke 8:43–45).

The crowd pressed in. The term Luke uses implies they were demanding and rude. When Jesus asked who had touched him, they all denied it. Humor leaps off the pages of this scene. An entire crowd is touching him and Jesus asks, "Who did it?" We can imagine everyone backing up and saying, "I didn't touch him; did you touch him?" "No. Did you?"

The sick woman watched from the crowd. Heartache, pain, and suffering described her life for the last twelve years. She had not known physical death, but social and ceremonial death. The law required that she not touch others and that she keep away from temple worship and public mingling. Any place she sat, touched, or laid would be unclean. Mark adds that "she had suffered a great deal under the care of many doctors and had spent all she had, yet instead of getting better she grew worse" (Mark 5:26). Culturally, the only thing worse than her condition was leprosy.

Her illness devastated her family and her social contacts. It stripped her of dignity and love. It squeezed joy out of her life.

We can often point to something specific that brings pain— we may smoke for forty years and get emphysema; we may have a football accident and suffer knee problems. On some level, we at least understand why. This woman had no concrete answers for why she suffered.

For twelve years questions haunted her: *Why me? Why am I considered unclean? Why can't my condition be cured?* Haven't we all asked why? *Why was I injured in a car wreck? There were hundreds of cars on the road that day. Why do I have cancer? I exercised regularly and took care of my body.*

For most people who suffer, the why question haunts. Christians may give superficial answers such as, "Well, it's just God's will," or "God is giving you this blessing; try to accept it and bring him glory in it." These are easy to say but difficult to hear. When people suffer, they do not ask why abstractly. They ask it personally, from the depths of their souls. They ask a person—Why, *God*?

Joni Eareckson Tada is a quadriplegic. She insists, "God . . . does not give advice. He does not give reasons or answers. He goes one better. He gives himself. . . . God wrote a book on suffering and he called it Jesus. This is why God is good. He is good because he gives himself."[7] The answer to suffering is a person, Jesus, to walk with us and sustain us.

Why do some people suffer more than others? Only God knows. In general, pain and suffering entered our world because of human freedom. God gave Adam and Eve a choice in the Garden of Eden, and they chose to rebel. We often think people will follow God if they live free from pain. But Adam and Eve lived in a pain-free world and still chose to rebel! Pain and suffering resulted from the fall.

Yet when it comes to punishment for specific acts of wrongdoing, the Bible states we don't have the right to judge another's suffering as a result of specific sin. In Luke 13, we have Jesus' most comprehensive response to suffering. The beginning of the chapter refers to a construction accident where a tower fell and senselessly killed eighteen people. Jesus said,

And those eighteen in Jerusalem the other day, the ones crushed and killed when the Tower of Siloam collapsed and fell on them, do you think they were worse citizens than all other Jerusalemites? Not at all. (Luke 13:4–5 Message)

Jesus assured them that those who died in the accident were not worse than those who lived. They were not being punished for their sins. In reality, Jesus did not directly address the why question. He said we should learn from this and live for God: "Unless you turn to God, you, too, will die" (Luke 13:5 Message).

The woman who touched Jesus had probably asked God "Why?" a thousand times. In that moment, she took a risk. She stepped out in faith. "She said to herself, 'If I only touch his cloak, I will be healed'" (Matt. 9:21). More accurately, she *kept saying* to herself that if she touched his cloak, she would be healed. She spoke words of faith, love, and hope to herself.

The words we speak to ourselves are very important. They shape our view of ourselves and our future. They mold our identity. This woman learned to speak things that would bolster her confidence and faith. When she extended her hand, she stretched beyond physical infirmities, cultural no-no's, and religious forbiddens. When she touched Jesus in faith, his power was released and she was healed.

In life, we have plenty of preexisting conditions and labels: college dropout, divorcée, bankrupt, addict, widow, orphan, has-been, loser, yuppie, hippie; the list could be endless. This woman's label was "unclean." In hospital ERs a preexisting condition can block one's insurance coverage. But in the ER of life there is no preexisting condition beyond Jesus' healing power; this woman reached for Jesus despite her condition! She touched him although she was untouchable, and discovered that God's love *covers*. No exclusions. No exceptions. No fine print. You're an alcoholic? It's covered. You're manic-depressive, heartbroken, grieving, or stressed out? It's covered. You're feeling like a failure as a parent, a student, an employee? It's covered.

Jesus said, "Someone touched me; I know that power has gone out from me" (Luke 8:46). I don't know if Jesus really didn't know who touched him. If he didn't, his Father in heaven did. God knew this woman's struggle, her faith, and her pain.

She must have felt terrified to step forward, for she had no idea how Jesus would respond. She trembled as she put one foot in front of the other, moving out from the crowd and falling at Jesus' feet. With courage she revealed to everyone her infirmity, why she had touched Jesus, and how she had been healed instantly. Her courage activated Jesus' power.

Jesus addressed this woman, saying, "Daughter, your faith has healed you. Go in peace" (Luke 8:48). She is the only person in the Bible designated by Jesus as "daughter." Her faith brought healing! The word *healed* derives from the word *salvation*. Jesus is offering her more than just physical healing; he is offering spiritual salvation. She is free to "go in peace" in both a physical and a spiritual sense. For the first time in twelve years a light has appeared in her darkness. God's power has rescued her from the depths of despair, and his love has brought healing to her brokenness.

Love's Resources

This is a beautiful story, but maybe it appears a little too clean-cut. What about when God does not heal? What about those who touch Jesus and continue to suffer? How can they deal with their pain?

I have little right to say much about this, considering that my only current symptom of pain is a chapped nose. Still,

I have learned much from talking with people who endure extreme pain. My work as a pastor has led me to people enduring pain at every level imaginable. Here is some of what I have learned from them.

When we are hurting, we can search out survivor stories. Many people who suffer from chronic pain share that they find connection and hope in others who deal with pain in a positive way. Survivors, they say, challenge their perspective and urge them to carry on. They suggest reading the stories of Reneé Bondi, Joni Eareckson Tada, or Tim Hansel; asking others whom they have been inspired by; and searching out stories of hope.

Psychologists and doctors have pointed out that the feeling of helplessness is one of the main destructive elements in dealing with pain. They suggest looking for ways to move your focus off the pain and contribute. For Reneé Bondi, it is music. For Joni Eareckson Tada, it is art. For Tim Hansel, it is writing. Many find strength by working and volunteering.

The Bible commands all of us, "Carry each other's burdens, and in this way you will fulfill the law of Christ" (Gal. 6:2). People who suffer receive hope as they encourage others along the way. Henri Nouwen said,

> There is great power in the mutual sharing of burdens. Those who can sit in silence with their fellowman, not knowing what to say but knowing that they should be there, can bring new life in a dying heart. Those who are not afraid to hold a hand in gratitude, to shed tears in grief, and to let a sigh of distress arise straight from the heart can break through paralyzing boundaries and witness the birth of a new fellowship, the fellowship of the broken.[8]

Who needs a listening ear? Who needs encouragement? Who needs help carrying a burden? God will not always heal, but he will respond to our prayers, and in that we can discover faith's peace.

Ultimate Healing

On a Monday evening in February, Tracy shaved his head. His wife, Dani, had shaved hers a few weeks before. For Tracy, it was a statement of solidarity and love. For Dani, it was inevitable: chemo would soon steal it anyway. A few weeks earlier, just before Christmas, they had heard the terrifying one-word diagnosis: cancer. Their world turned upside down. Two years earlier, doctors had discovered a tumor on Dani's neck, which they treated. However, two years later they learned that the cancer had metastasized to her bones and liver.

Over the next three months Dani received treatments. Good days and difficult days passed; at times she felt excruciating pain. Though Dani maintained a joyous attitude, the wear to her body was evident.

Dani walked the painful road of cancer with amazing courage and hope. The entire family rallied. Their courage inspired others, and many prayed for God to spare this young mother of two children.

Dani said,

> We talked about the "why" questions. One thing that was brought up was that this may not be for us; this may not be for our children. This may be for someone we don't even know. We came to the conclusion that we would walk the walk Christ wanted us to walk. We would do what Jesus wanted and show love to all those we came in contact with. We would let people know that there is hope.[9]

They realized that God's purposes are far beyond the immediate and apparent. They trusted in the presence of Christ in the midst of pain. They reached out to Jesus and clung to the hem of his garment. If ever a family lived with faith and love, it was theirs.

Eventually, Dani's cancer went into remission. It seemed that God had answered our prayers. Yet after writing this chapter, I learned that Dani's cancer had returned fiercely and unexpectedly. Despite the doctors' efforts, she passed away.

Before Dani's death Tracy said, "Her healing may not be physical healing. God will heal everybody eventually. Because when we go to be with him we will be healed forever. You may not be healed on this earth, but you will be healed."[10] In that sense she was healed. God did answer prayer, but not in the way we anticipated. Jesus' peace is all that sustained this family through difficult days.

Peace in the Storm

The peace Jesus offers is greater than our current suffering; it allows us to carry on through trying times. Paul calls it the "peace of God, which transcends all understanding," and he prays that peace "will guard your hearts and your minds in Christ Jesus" (Phil. 4:7). My heart still sinks for Tracy. Tears still come. He and his family still grieve. I wish I could take their pain away, your pain away. I wish I could heal it and erase its negative effects. I can't. But God makes his presence available. He will walk with you and sustain you even through the darkest valley.

In the book of Mark we read about a day when Jesus' disciples were out on the sea. A fierce storm arose. Winds howled and waves crashed, filling the boat with water. Terrified, the disciples tried to keep their boat afloat.

They became exasperated when they realized that Jesus was sleeping at the stern of the boat. Waking him, they asked,

"Lord, do you not care if we die?" In other words, "Don't you care that we are suffering and we are in danger? Does it matter to you that we hurt and perish?" That is the question of pain.

I feel the sting of the disciples' question. It is a question I ponder at every funeral and one I revisit after spending time with a family at a hospice. But the story does not end there. Jesus walked to the front of the boat and looked out at the crashing waves. He stared right into the storm and rebuked it, saying, "Peace, be still!" (Mark 4:39 NKJV). Literally he said, "Be muzzled," and suddenly the wind stopped and the sea looked as still as glass. He turned to his disciples and said, "Why are you so afraid? Do you still have no faith?"

Does God care? Yes. There is much I don't understand about why we suffer, but he cares. He gives us something better than answers; he gives himself. One day he will speak peace to all pain. The Bible promises that a day will come when God will "wipe every tear from their eyes. There will be no more death or mourning or crying or pain, for the old order of things has passed away" (Rev. 21:4). The roller coaster will finally come to a stop. Until then, hold on tight to your faith. Invite Jesus to walk out and speak to your storm, "Peace, be still."

QUESTIONS FOR DISCUSSION

1. Did you ever think that all pain would go away after you became a Christian?
2. In what ways can pain be positive?
3. Discuss Joni Eareckson Tada's statement, "God . . . does not give advice. He does not give reasons or answers. He goes one better. He gives himself. . . . God

wrote a book on suffering and he called it Jesus. This is why God is good. He is good because he gives himself."

4. Read Luke 13:1–5 for Jesus' most comprehensive explanation of suffering and sin. What does this tell us about the connection between pain and specific sin?

5. What has helped you deal with pain?

6. What are some practical ways you and your church can bring healing to others?

5

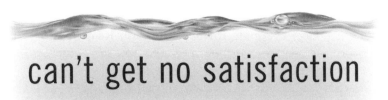

can't get no satisfaction

One day your life will flash before your eyes. Make sure it is worth watching.

Anonymous

We live in a world obsessed with success. Maybe that's why I get a kick out of an organization called Demotivators that spoofs all of our success slogans. Their slogan is "Increasing success by lowering expectations." Here are some of their demotivating sayings:

Mediocrity: It takes a lot less time and most people won't notice the difference until it's too late.

Regret: It hurts to admit when you make mistakes—but when they're big enough, the pain only lasts a second.

Persistence: It's over, man. Let her go.

Wish: When you wish upon a star, your dreams can come true, unless it is really a meteorite hurling to earth that will destroy all life. Then you are pretty much hosed no matter what you wish for, unless it is death by meteorite. **Success**: Some people dream of success, while other people live to crush those dreams.[1]

Success is an American icon. We strive to be successful and are encouraged to give our lives, time, and energy to the idol of success. But what does it really mean to be a successful person? Peggy Noonan, former President Reagan's speechwriter and someone in the upper echelons of power, said:

> Success is nice and I've had some and enjoyed it, but so what? It isn't sufficient reason to get up in the morning. It's not good enough to live for. Success for me has been, essentially, getting invited to things I don't want to go to but like saying I went to. . . . Oddly enough, whenever I have been at the center of things in the White House, at the party, in the studio, I would enjoy them and have a great time and notice things, but I would also think . . . this is all an illusion. This is a lovely, tender illusion. We're all running around being busy and doing important things but this has nothing to do with anything. Up there God and the angels are looking down and laughing, and not unkindly. They just find us touching and dizzy.[2]

Around all of that power, Noonan sensed a greater power that dwarfed her own. Success must be more than power.

For a lot of people fame equals success. As a teen I desired nothing more than to be a rock star. I played "air guitar" in front of the mirror, working on my moves for the day when the cameras would be on me. That day never came. And I'm thankful. Watch any episode of *True Hollywood Stories* or *Biography* or VH1's *Behind the Music* and see how disastrous fame can be. Every story sounds the same as celebrities pour out their pain. Success is surely more than fame.

According to Wall Street, money is the currency of success. I love the scene in the film *Forrest Gump* when Forrest realizes he is a millionaire, and he doesn't have to worry about money. He comments, "That's good. One less thing."³

What is success that truly satisfies? Are you tired of chasing after dreams that leave you empty? Sick of long workweeks with little to show for it? Bummed at the thought that your current life is all it will ever be? These questions caught up to a hard Jewish man named Zacchaeus who had felt that mixture of success and despair. He had it all and it wasn't enough, but when he encountered Jesus he discovered the true meaning of success.

God Evasion

Zacchaeus was the chief tax collector, head of the Jericho IRS. He maintained a powerful position in the Roman government because of Jericho's unique position as a central trading route. He supervised other tax collectors. Though his name means "pure" and "innocent," he was neither.

The people of Israel felt strongly about taxes and tax collectors. Tax collectors stopped people on the road and demanded tax payment based on the value of their goods. The system was regulated, but the collector had the freedom to overvalue goods and tax accordingly. The opportunity for fraud was enormous, thus the tax collectors' reputation. Also, tax collectors stood as a symbol of Roman rule and authority, a reminder the Israelites loathed. The tax collector's role was so despised that it regularly appears in the Bible alongside terms like "prostitutes" and "sinners" (see Matt. 21:31–32; Mark 2:15). Jews hated taxes.

Not much has changed in two thousand years. We don't like taxes today either. Consider these bumper stickers:

"Born free . . . taxed to death."
"The Lottery: A tax on people who are bad at math."
"IRS: We've got what it takes to take what you've got."

We fret because we pay taxes to support our own government. Imagine the climate if we paid taxes to a nation ruling over us. That is the frustration the Israelites had. It is no wonder that when Jesus came to Jericho the crowd refused to let this tax collector through to see him. They didn't budge.

Zacchaeus couldn't see beyond the person in front of him. He was very short, which may have contributed to his ruthless pursuit of wealth; his feelings of inferiority may have motivated him to reach for greater levels of social power. "So he ran ahead and climbed a sycamore-fig tree to see him, since Jesus was coming that way" (Luke 19:4).

Why does Luke insist on telling us he climbed a sycamore-fig tree? One expert sheds some light: "The branches of the sycamore-fig tree are strong and wide spreading, and because it produces many lateral branches, it was an easy tree for Zacchaeus to climb in which he could easily be hidden."[4] Zacchaeus did not want to be seen, but he did want to see Jesus. He searched, but he also hid.

We do the same thing with God. We may hide in drugs or alcohol or an addiction. Perhaps we get lost in distractions. Passion for one's work can become a ready hiding place as we become so consumed with work we make no time for God. Not much has changed since childhood—we are still masters of hide-and-seek. Only now the excitement and anticipation of being found are anything but fun.

We often think of those who hide from God as people outside the faith. But I believe there are equally as many people hiding from God within our churches and religious institutions; they are like Zacchaeus—they want to see, but they don't want to be seen. They may hide out of fear of rejection. Leaving the shadows of addiction or pain is terrifying. Coming clean with God and others about our true struggles, doubts, and concerns remains a tender and delicate thing. If our trust has broken down with God, or if we imagine him to be unloving, the fear of rejection can paralyze us.

Others hide because of insecurity. Henri Nouwen claims the greatest struggle of Christians is self-rejection, the tendency to see oneself in a negative way.[5] Because of this tendency we fall prey to the allure of success, power, and fame. We seek to establish our worth through those avenues. In all our efforts to "prove" our value, we remain in the shadows about who we really are. Rather than bring our whole selves into the light and love of God, we feel much better about our "Sunday" selves. But this is a cover-up for our own insecurities.

Sometimes we hide because we have been hurt. We dreamt of how our lives would go after we became Christians. We thought our problems would just go away, or at least lessen. But to our dismay the challenges of life increased. We began to pull back into hiding. Maybe we were hurt in ministry as a volunteer or a pastor. The criticisms we endured still sting, and our wounds are still sore. Coming out of that we may resign ourselves to a new Christian experience: we will still attend church and we will see Jesus, but without him having anything to do with us. We want to see and not be seen. There are many ways we play hide-and-seek. Do we need to reopen our hearts to the relentless love of God? Is it time to bring our secret sins out of the shadows and into the light?

Zacchaeus was acquainted with hide-and-seek. As a tax man, he knew there were those who hid from him, trying to evade their taxes. As a Jew, he knew what it meant to hide from God. But Jesus searched him out and called him down from that sycamore-fig tree to face an audit that would alter his life forever.

Life Audit

Webster's dictionary defines an audit as "a methodical examination and review." Most Americans fear a tax audit. We're afraid we didn't put the right numbers on the right line, and we'll have to pay for it. As Jesus came to the place where Zacchaeus hid in the tree, he "looked up and said to him, 'Zacchaeus, come down immediately. I must stay at your house today.' So he came down at once and welcomed him gladly. All the people saw this and began to mutter, 'He has gone to be the guest of a "sinner"'" (Luke 19:5–7).

This appointment was more than just a meal. Zacchaeus, familiar with ancient tax audits, underwent a love audit in Christ's presence. Rather than have a terrifying experience, he would be challenged by Jesus' love and compassion.

Luke tells us people were scandalized that Jesus would eat with a sinner like Zacchaeus. Jesus often hung out with those outside of the religious mainstream and had great compassion for them. In fact, the number one emotional response of Jesus mentioned in the Gospels is compassion.[6] This is astounding when we consider that Jesus was sinless but was constantly surrounded by sin and sinful people. Sin violently opposed his character. Everywhere he turned he saw the effects of evil and unrighteousness. It would have been easy for Jesus to blast people for their mistakes. He had more right than anyone to take a political and moral stand, picket on the street, form protests, and publicly attack individuals for their sins. Yet we read that when Jesus "saw the crowds, he had compassion on them, because they were harassed and helpless, like sheep without a shepherd" (Matt. 9:36).

"Harassed" carries the idea of being jerked, hurled, or thrown down. It originally meant flayed or mangled, but it became equivalent to being overwhelmed with weariness. Jesus saw people as sheep who have been bruised, beaten, and thrown to and fro. He was filled with love rather than disdain.

People are not always easy to love, and Jesus knew this. Though their actions brought out the compassion of Jesus, they also reduced him to a gut-wrenching sigh. Mark tells us that "the Pharisees came and began to question Jesus. To test him, they asked him for a sign from heaven. He sighed deeply and said, 'Why does this generation ask for a miraculous sign? I tell you the truth, no sign will be given to it'" (Mark 8:11–12). The text goes on to say that he simply got back in a boat and crossed the Sea of Galilee. He was deeply distressed by the stubborn hearts of the Pharisees and the lack of love in the masses (see Mark 3:4–5).

On this particular day, Jesus saw Zacchaeus hiding and he called him out of the shadows with compassion. During their meal Zacchaeus realized that while he had made a lot of money, he wasn't truly happy. He had fed his ego and insecurities, but his vision of success excluded God and came up empty.

True Success

When Zacchaeus encountered Jesus, he discovered true success in God's love. People have given many definitions of success, some of which are very helpful. Webster's defines success as: "(1) a favorable result; (2) the gaining of wealth, fame, etc." Success may mean many different things, but behind success that truly satisfies lies the key ingredient: love. All the degrees we earn are meaningless without love. All the toys we collect and enjoy are void without love. All the accolades and honors we acquire are empty without love.

As we come out of our personal shadows, we accept ourselves as those radically loved by God. In that acceptance, we begin to view others similarly. We see them with compassion and mercy.

In Mark 12, a religious teacher questioned Jesus by asking a commonly debated religious question: What is the greatest commandment? At some level, this question is about spiritual success. What is the essential thing that would equal spiritual success?

There were 613 commands and innumerable oral traditions to choose from; the answer did not appear simple. According to Jewish teaching there were 248 affirmative laws, one for every part of the human body, and 365 negative laws, one for each day of the year. The laws were divided into heavy and light, the heavy ones being absolutely binding and the light ones less binding. So this teacher assumed that however Jesus answered, he could show him up and win the debate.

But Jesus answered that the most important commandment was to "'Love the Lord your God with all your heart and with all your soul and with all your mind and with all your strength.' The second is this: 'Love your neighbor as yourself.' There is no commandment greater than these" (Mark 12:30–31). Out of our love for God we are empowered to love one another.

I would love to have seen that teacher's face! Jesus responded with the most copied passage in all of Judaism. It is part of the Shema, the Hebrew word for "hear," and every faithful Jew recited the Shema twice a day. The religious teacher was left humbled without any ammunition. The text sums this section up by saying, "From then on no one dared ask him any more questions" (v. 34). It doesn't take a rocket scientist to realize that if you debate the Son of God, you will lose.

If we have love, we have success. As Charles Milak said, "Success is neither fame, wealth, nor power; rather it is seeking, knowing, loving, and obeying God. If you seek, you will know; if you know, you will love; if you love, you will obey."[7] This is a far cry from the world's version of success. People say: get all you can no matter what. Jesus says: live generously and God will supply your needs. People say: flaunt your accomplishment and boast of your ability. Jesus says: live humbly and take up your cross. People say: show me the money! Jesus says: you cannot serve both God and money.

All our effort is not enough without God. Fame and wealth are not bad in and of themselves, but they can be fatal when we buy into our own press reports. When I experience success, I am tempted to look in the mirror and make it all about me. Every time I do, I fall flat on my face. God has a way of humbling me! I usually have to repeat this process multiple times before I get it.

In moments of success I tend to forget how frail, weak, and sinful I am. I also forget that despite any achievements, the Bible remains clear that I have sinned and fallen short of God's glory. This is why I believe success is much more difficult to handle than failure. The truly successful, however, realize that all success is by the grace of God, and they grow in love for God and others.

The church often holds up models of success that are no different from the world's models. Yet Jesus is calling us to a new life, a new reality, and therefore, a new perspective on where success is found and what success means. The cliché is true: nobody on their deathbed wishes they had spent more time at the office. Success at the end of life is more about love, integrity, and relationships than accolades. If that is true of the end of our lives, shouldn't it be true each day?

Zacchaeus had swindled and devalued people for years, but as he experienced the love of God, his perspective changed radically. Zacchaeus came up short in his audit; he was a sinner in need of grace. He endured a sweeping shakeup. After lunch he said to Jesus, "Look, Lord! Here and now I give half of my possessions to the poor, and if I have cheated anybody out of anything, I will pay back four times the amount" (Luke 19:8). Talk about a power lunch! He came out of this deal a new person, changed by the grace and the power of Jesus Christ. He discovered something that satisfied much more than money did.

Lifestyles of the Not So Rich and Famous

How can you succeed ultimately?

Real success starts with honesty, because no significant life change happens without it. King David learned this the hard way. After David had an affair with Bathsheba and arranged her husband's death, Nathan the prophet visited him. Nathan told him a story about a rich man with many sheep and cattle and a poor man with one lamb. The man loved the lamb as if it were his own daughter. One day a guest came to visit the rich man. Since the rich man didn't want to use his own livestock, he took the poor man's only lamb and had it slaughtered to provide for his guest.

When David heard this story he burned with anger. He claimed, "As surely as the LORD lives, the man who did this deserves to die!" (2 Sam. 12:5). "Then Nathan said to David, 'You are the man!'" (v. 7). When the truth sank in, David came clean and said, "I have sinned against the LORD" (v. 13). This scene from David's life reveals our amazing ability to justify, rationalize, and brush away our sin.

True success requires honesty with self and with God. One can't be successful playing games with God. Sometimes the best way I get honest with myself is to ask myself the hard questions and then compare my answers with those of a trusted friend. My friend sees me "from the outside" and can comment on certain areas of behavioral patterns that may need to be altered.

Another way we experience success is to choose to cheat the right things. What is most important in life? After Zacchaeus' love audit he willingly paid back everyone he owed and surrendered that part of his life. God became his priority, and success involved being right with God and others.

Jesus says, "For where your treasure is, there your heart will be also" (Matt. 6:21). He doesn't say, "Where your heart is, there your treasure is." One's heart follows one's treasure. Jesus' teaching reveals the same principle the mysterious Watergate informant told reporters: "Follow the money." When you follow the money in your own life, what do you find? Where does it go? Are you stressed to the breaking point over finances? Do you find that you waste most of your time and energy worrying about debt issues rather than loving others? Do you need to re-prioritize?

The issue is not about being rich or poor, it is about priorities and who rules our lives. John Templeton is an investment legend. He made millions, was featured on *Lifestyles of the Rich and Famous*, and traveled the world. But Templeton remained faithful to a biblical vision of success. He established the Templeton Prize for Progress in Religion, the largest religious cash prize in the world. He advocated a double tithe for himself to God's kingdom and has given untold monies to further God's work. *Forbes* said of him, "Unlike most of us, Templeton is at peace with himself. He has sorted things out."[8] He has kept God and people as the priority.

Zacchaeus cheated God and others morally and financially. That may not be your struggle. Perhaps you are a dedicated Christian, but you are involved in so many things and activities at church that you have no time for your family. Your children may dislike church because they feel neglected because of it. The first ministry you are called to is your family.

I love the message my friend Andy Stanley gives called "Choosing to Cheat." The core idea is that we all have to choose to cheat somewhere, whether it is with our children, our work, our church, our health, or our spouse. The question isn't, "Will I cheat?" but "What is the right thing to cheat?"

This became critical for me at a time when I was neglecting my wife and kids for ministry work. Andy helped me realize that while I could be replaced as a pastor, the only place I remained categorically unique in this world was at home. I am the only husband and father my family will ever have. Every other place in life I am dispensable, but in my home I am absolutely essential.[9] I had to choose between better and best. I had to become willing to say no to some great things so I could agree to do the best things. It is hard to reprioritize, but it is the pathway to discover true success in what matters most.

After Zacchaeus' claim to reform, Jesus said, "Today salvation has come to this house, because this man, too, is a son of Abraham. For the Son of Man came to seek and to save what was lost" (Luke 19:9–10).

Zacchaeus was free! Free from sin, free from emptiness, and free from the pain that his success had brought him. Despite the fact that he was, in Frederick Buechner's words, a "sawed-off little social disaster with a big bank account and a crooked job . . . Jesus welcomes him aboard anyway."[10] That's the awesome thing about Jesus; he welcomes us in spite of our past, our sins, our mistakes. Zacchaeus surrendered to God and discovered where ultimate success was found.

Sports legend and NFL Network commentator Deion Sanders put it this way: "Success almost ruined my life, but thank God, I came to Him just in the nick of time. And that has made all the difference."[11]

I'm all for healthy success. I love to see people achieve their dreams. I enjoy watching others succeed, both relationally and materially—but not at the expense of their spiritual well-being. Has success almost ruined your life? Let Jesus call you out of that sycamore-fig tree, out of that place of hiding, out of that addiction or broken marriage or troubled work situation. Let him satisfy your heart's desires.

QUESTIONS FOR DISCUSSION

1. What does it mean to be successful in our society?
2. How does the Bible define success?
3. Zacchaeus wanted to see God but did not want to be seen. In what ways do people play hide-and-seek from God?
4. Jesus, the most spiritually mature person ever, remained approachable to sinners and outsiders. What can we learn from that?
5. What are some practical ways you or your church can remain open to outsiders?
6. Are there areas you should "choose to cheat" so you can succeed in more important ones?

6

hugging the cactus

The symbol of the cross in the church points to the God who was crucified not between two candles on an altar, but between two thieves in the place of the skull, where the outcasts belong, outside the gates of the city.

Jürgen Moltmann

Actor Mel Gibson has dominated the headlines for all the wrong reasons in the last several years. His mug shot has been posted all over the world for drunk driving, racial slurs, marital drama, and anger issues. Since making *The Passion of the Christ*, he's become known more for disturbing passion than Christ.

That's why I loved watching a recent YouTube clip of Robert Downey Jr. giving an acceptance speech for an acting award he received. He asked Mel to introduce him, but Mel didn't know Robert was setting him up.

After the introduction, Robert's speech had little to do with himself and everything to do with Mel. He talked about his own well-documented addiction and how Mel counseled him to lean into his faith and find forgiveness. Mel cast Robert in a movie that was originally developed for himself, and allowed Robert to keep working and pay the bills at one of his lowest points when nobody else would hire him.

Robert said Mel told him,

If I accepted responsibility for my wrongdoings, if I embraced that part of my soul that was ugly, "hugging the cactus," he calls it . . . I'd become a man of some humility and my life would take on new meaning. And I did and it worked. All he asked in return is that someday I help the next guy in some small way. It is reasonable to assume that at the time he didn't imagine the next guy would be him. . . . On this special occasion . . . I humbly ask that you join me . . . in forgiving my friend his trespasses, offering him the same clean slate you have me, and allowing him to continue his great and ongoing contribution to our collective art without shame. He's hugged the cactus long enough.[1]

The crowd erupted in applause.

I loved watching Robert stand by his friend when it seemed the whole world was appalled at him. That act of loyalty and deference led to a rousing ovation that would have been inconceivable only moments before.

The astounding thing about the Christian faith is that forgiveness and love are possible because Jesus hugged the cactus for us. Yes, there are times when we too must hug the cactus in order to learn life's lessons. But the message of the gospel is that we don't have to stay there. We can move on in the light and love of Jesus.

One man who knew what it was to hug the cactus experienced Jesus' love in a moment that changed the world. He met Jesus on a hillside, hanging on a cross next to him. Accused and condemned, this anonymous thief was thrown together with Jesus in this horrific scene. They endured torture side by side at Golgotha, which means the "place of the skull."

The thief was a forgotten person outside a small city in an even smaller country. His appearance was appalling, his mistakes condemning, his rap sheet long. We would be tempted to say he was a worthless man deserving punishment. Yet that day he reached out to Jesus and found love and grace.

Rebel Love

Only a week earlier people had praised and worshiped Jesus as he rode into Jerusalem. But the mob was fickle. On Friday the same people who had praised him betrayed him.

By the time Jesus arrived at the cross, he had endured six trials, or hearings, in under eighteen hours. The first three trials were Jewish. The second three were Roman. These trials violated most rules of Roman and Jewish law. Mark Moore lists several points that catalog the breaches of justice in Jesus' trials:

1. He was arrested through a bribe (i.e., blood money).
2. He was arrested without a clear charge.
3. Trials could not be held at night or on feast days.
4. The religious establishment used physical force to try to intimidate Jesus during the trial.
5. False witnesses offered conflicting testimony against him.
6. Witnesses were not supposed to testify in the presence of each other.

7. Jesus was asked to incriminate himself, which he really didn't do!

8. Jesus was not given the opportunity to cross-examine the witnesses.

9. The high priest never asked for a vote from the Sanhedrin, which should have started with the youngest and gone to the oldest.

10. He [Jesus] was charged with blasphemy and temple violation at his Jewish trial, but the charges were changed at his civil trial to claiming to be king, causing disturbances, and refusing to pay taxes.

11. He was convicted and executed the same day as his trial.[2]

Jesus' trial was a mockery of justice. Pilate, the leading authority, did not want him to die, so he had him severely whipped in hopes this would sway the crowd.

The Romans were masters of torture. Before crucifixion, they flogged the victim by using whips with pieces of bone and glass knotted into them; this ripped and mutilated the victim's flesh. Both Jesus and the thieves endured this treatment. Their arms were tied to a post, and they were stripped and beaten down the back, buttocks, and legs. Such a flogging took the life of a victim six out of ten times. If a victim survived, he was often carried out on a stretcher.

Jesus' flogging was severe. Peter says, "He himself bore our sins in his body on the tree, so that we might die to sins and live for righteousness; by his wounds you have been healed" (1 Pet. 2:24). The term *wounds* refers to bloody and bruising blows inflicted upon slaves in that era. The term suggests Jesus was beaten particularly hard, possibly more than the traditional thirty-nine lashes, due to the accusation that he had claimed to be king.

After Jesus' flogging, the soldiers shoved the crown of thorns on his head. By the time he walked to Calvary, he was probably in shock due to the pain and the blood loss.[3] He carried the seventy-five to one hundred pound crossbar on his back.

At Calvary, the vertical posts would have been permanently set. The victim would be laid on his back and his wrists nailed to the crossbeam. Traditional Christian art suggests the nails were driven into the palms, but archaeological and scientific evidence point to the nail going through the wrists. The palm of the hand could not support the weight of a body without ripping out. Biblical writers would have seen the wrist as part of the larger area of one's hands. The spikes through Jesus' wrists would have damaged the median nerve, sending unbelievable jolts of pain through his body.

After the soldiers drove the spikes into his hands at Calvary, they raised him into position and nailed his feet. The spikes in his feet would also have damaged nerves and increased the torture. He heard taunting from several groups. Matthew tells us passersby shouted insults, shaking their heads and saying, "You who are going to destroy the temple and build it in three days, save yourself! Come down from the cross, if you are the Son of God!" (Matt. 27:40). The populace, like puppets, repeated the verdict of their leaders.

The religious leaders stood back in assurance of this victory for God. They would rid the world of this rebel; they would free the people from his lies. If he really was the Son of God, they reasoned, he would save himself. Since he had not, they must be right! I imagine a look of cool satisfaction as they said, "Let him come down now from the cross, and we will believe in him" (Matt. 27:42). If Jesus had come down, they would only have nailed him back up on the cross! They had heard of Lazarus rising from the dead, but that knowledge had not affected them.

Crucifixion is a gruesome way to die. To say its equivalent today would be the gas chamber or the electric chair is too tame. These modern ways of executing people, as horrible as they are, have become sterile and sanitized compared to crucifixion. They are private, where crucifixion was public; they are quick, where crucifixion would take many hours. In fact, the concept of crucifixion was so gruesome that the Gospel writers give no detail other than the one-word description—crucified. They don't tell us anything about how Jesus was crucified. One word in that era painted the picture of horror. Jesus suffered so intensely, and his followers sympathized so deeply, they could not bring themselves to mention it in any but the briefest terms.

Early Christians had many symbols. They depicted the church as Noah's ark, saving those inside from destruction. They drew the dove to symbolize the Holy Spirit as mentioned in Acts. Jesus is shown as the Good Shepherd tending to his sheep, and we see many accounts of the Last Supper.[4] But nowhere do we see the symbol of the cross. The first cross appears to have been carved in a door of the Church of Santa Sabina in the fifth century, over a hundred years after crucifixion had been made illegal.[5] A full four hundred years were required to forget the horror enough for people to use it as a symbol of faith.

Time and distance have transformed the cross into a fashion statement. One catalog now features crosses for sale: "Look at the trendy, beautiful people walking down the fashion runways, and check out what they are wearing around their necks. . . . This sterling silver cross necklace. Chunky sterling silver cross with a glittering cubic zirconium in the center, strung on the sterling silver box chain."[6]

Jesus did not die on a pretty silver cross; yet that cross represents the height of love. He could have stepped down

104

and walked away. He could have refused to die. But in that moment he laid it all down so that we could be saved. He did it all for love.

How strange it is that we glorify the cross. We wear it as jewelry and place it in our churches. This symbol of legalized torture became the primary symbol of the Christian faith. Someone wrote, "I wonder if the Romans had chosen to hang, or to behead, or to mutilate, or to shoot, would we sing of the precious old rope? Would we talk of the sweet machete, or the blessed 357 Magnum? Think about the moving factor of Christ's love. Christ's love changes everything it touches, even a tool to execute someone."

His love transformed those crossbeams into the very place where God's justice and forgiveness met. Those crossbeams make heavy burdens bearable, long hours manageable, and ordinary faces beautiful. They turn service into joy, friends into family, and houses into homes. That's God's love. And it all culminated there, when Jesus died so that we might live.

Nietzsche saw the paradox of Jesus hanging on a cross as a horrible inversion of all classical thought on God. The cross turned everything upside down. The Greek gods knew little of humility or serving one another. Christianity's "god on a cross" created a "revaluation of all the values of antiquity."[7] He saw this as a terrible thing, but the beauty of the Christian faith is precisely its contrast to the Greek gods. Those gods were shaped after man's image. The love seen in the cross is God in the flesh, changing everything and turning it upside down!

Antiques Roadshow

Millions of Americans tune in to *Antiques Roadshow*. We watch in amazement when seventy-eight-year-old Ethel from Waxahache shows up with an old wooden box her grandfather gave her. It is appraised at $30,000. "I had no idea," she says. "It just sat in our garage for years."

Antiques Roadshow makes me look at items in my garage differently. I see an old metal pipe and wonder, "Hey, maybe that is Civil War steel! Maybe that's worth a few thousand bucks."

The principle *Antiques Roadshow* teaches is this: never judge value by appearance. An article may be old and decrepit but worth thousands of dollars. Value is determined by what someone pays for it. Even at *Antiques Roadshow*, a piece isn't actually worth $20,000 unless someone pays $20,000 for it. Appearances may be deceiving.

The cross declares that God values people so much he was willing to pay the price of his very Son for them. You and I will not lock eyes with anyone this week who does not matter deeply to God. They may appear worn and torn; they may be beaten up by society, by sin, and by hard times. They may be broken, but God already declared their inner worth to be astounding. As on *Antiques Roadshow*, appearance is deceiving. God's love sees deeper.

Opinions abound on what love is. I went with a camera crew down to Venice Beach in Southern California and asked people, "What does love mean to you?" They responded:

"Love is when it flushes over you and you fall into this euphoria with another person. There is nothing else and you do everything for them."

"Love is when you care about something more than you care about yourself."

"Love means you feel happy."

John writes, "This is how we know what love is: Jesus Christ laid down his life for us. And we ought to lay down our lives for our brothers" (1 John 3:16). The cross literally defines love. Without the cross we would not know what love really is. We may experience love in our lives and see glimpses of it, but the cross is the only act of pure love performed without the slightest hint of false motives in world history.[8]

John gets more definite a few verses later and writes, "This is love: not that we loved God, but that he loved us and sent his Son as an atoning sacrifice for our sins" (1 John 4:10). The most important issue is not our own love but God's love for us. Without the cross we would see evil in the world and be tempted to believe God does not love us. But there stands the cross. I may not understand fully why suffering and evil pervade our world, but I can look at the cross and find comfort in God's response. If God's own Son endured such hardship for me, why should I expect a life free from suffering? And I know that Jesus' death on the cross secured for me an eternity without pain.

Paul writes about the depth of God's love in the book of Romans. He said, "But God demonstrates his own love for us in this: While we were still sinners, Christ died for us" (5:8). Throughout Romans 5 Paul calls us "helpless," "ungodly," "sinners," and "enemies," yet while we were still all of these things, Christ died for us.

God not only demonstrates that love *historically* in the cross, he demonstrates it *experientially* through the Holy Spirit. As Paul writes, "God has poured out his love into our hearts by the Holy Spirit, whom he has given us" (v. 5). Jesus was not a random victim of a senseless death; he went to the cross as part of God's plan.

Kahlil Gibran, a brilliant poet and writer, captured the courage and power of Jesus' act when he wrote these words years ago on Good Friday:

Oh, Crucified Jesus . . . Thou art, on the Cross, more glorious and dignified than one thousand kings upon one thousand thrones in one thousand empires. . . .

Thou art, in the agony of death, more powerful than one thousand generals in one thousand wars. . . .

Forgive them, for they do not know that Thou hast conquered death with death, and bestowed life upon the dead. . . .

Forgive them, for they do not know Thy strength still awaits them. . . .

Forgive them, for they do not know that every day is Thy day.[9]

Sides of the Cross

On the cross, between two thieves, Jesus divided humanity. One criminal died the way he lived, hurling insults at Jesus. His last recorded words were spoken with a taunting attitude: "Aren't you the Christ? Save yourself and us!" (Luke 23:39). Even on his cross, this condemned man found the energy to mock Jesus. A person dying the most horrible death known to civilization wasted his final moments scorning the Son of God.

But the other criminal suddenly had a change of heart. He rebuked the other man for mocking Jesus and said, "'Don't you fear God . . . since you are under the same sentence? We are punished justly, for we are getting what our deeds deserve. But this man has done nothing wrong.' Then he said, 'Jesus, remember me when you come into your kingdom'" (vv. 40–42).

This thief may have grown up on the streets, or he may have been abused. Perhaps he had been in and out of jail most of his life. Maybe he had a good home life and just made bad choices. He couldn't stand on his past accomplishments or achievements. He had not lived faithfully before God. But

God set a divine appointment with him on that hill. This thief chose life. The fact that he asked Jesus to remember him, even though it was beyond doubt they were both about to die, was an amazing statement of faith.

Jesus responded to the thief's request, "I tell you the truth, today you will be with me in paradise" (v. 43). Those words changed everything for this man. Suddenly, even in the midst of death, love appeared. In the most hopeless situation imaginable, the promise of paradise came. What could be more unlike paradise than violence, blood, nails, and angry faces? Yet that very day Jesus extended his love and promise.

This scene typified humanity. One chose to believe, the other did not. One chose love, the other hate. One chose hope, the other despair. One chose life, the other death. Which side of the cross we are on depends on our choice about Jesus. "Father, forgive them," Jesus prayed from the cross, "they don't know what they are doing." He said, in essence, "I love you." How will we respond?

We are overwhelmed with choices today. I recently stood in the deodorant aisle for five minutes. Did I want regular deodorant, or sport, or sport extra, or sport cool breeze, or sport cool breeze in a blue bar or a green can? I bought three different kinds.

When I got home my wife asked me, "Why did you buy three different kinds?"

"I'm just trying them out," I said. This was true, but I also couldn't make up my mind. It's easy to get exhausted from making choices, but few choices really matter. In fact, much of our lives are spent working out the consequences of a few major choices. And only one choice marks the difference between life and death. Only one choice holds consequences for all others—what do I believe about Jesus? Which side of the cross am I on?

Leo Tolstoy described his own conversion in relation to the thief on the cross:

> I, like that thief on the cross, have believed Christ's teaching and been saved. And this is no far-fetched comparison, but the closest expression of the condition of spiritual despair and horror at the problem of life and death in which I lived formerly, and of the condition of peace and happiness in which I am now. I, like the thief, knew that I had lived and was living badly. . . . I, like the thief, knew that I was unhappy and suffering. . . . I, like the thief to the cross, was nailed by some force to that life of suffering and evil. And as, after the meaningless sufferings and evils of life, the thief awaited the terrible darkness of death, so did I await the same thing. . . . And suddenly I heard the words of Christ and understood them, and life and death ceased to seem to me evil, and instead of despair I experienced happiness and the joy of life undisturbed by death.[10]

And so Tolstoy, like the thief before him, experienced a radical love and learned to rest in that love.

The Death Chamber

If the ancient symbol of death was the cross, then the death chamber is our modern one. Karla Faye Tucker also learned to rest in God's love while strapped to a gurney in the death chamber. She comforted herself as she hummed. Moments earlier she had uttered a prayer, "Lord Jesus, help them to find my vein."

Fifteen years earlier Karla Faye Tucker and Danny Garret entered the apartment of Jerry Lynn Dean and Deborah Thornton around 3:00 a.m. Strung out on drugs, they had planned to steal a motorcycle. When they left the apartment they were guilty of two horrific murders with a pickax.

Karla Faye Tucker became a Christian between the time she committed the crime and her trial. Jury deliberation took a total of only seventy minutes.

Looking toward the window from the death chamber, she said, "I would like to say to all of you—the Thornton family and Jerry Dean's family—that I am so sorry. I hope God will give you peace with this."

She told her husband, Dana, "Baby, I love you."

To her friends she said, "Ron, give Peggy a hug for me. Everybody has been so good to me. I love all of you very much. I'm going to be face to face with Jesus now. Warden Baggett, thank you so much. You have been so good to me. I love all of you very much. I will see you all when you get there. I will wait for you."[11] After her final words she waited for the lethal injection.

The previous month Larry King interviewed Karla before millions on TV. At the end of the interview he said, "Finally, you remain up."

"Yes," she said.

He asked her to explain and added, "It can't just be God."

Smiling, Karla replied, "Yes, it can. It's called the joy of the Lord. When you've done something like I've done, and you've been forgiven for it and you're loved—that has a way of so changing you. I have experienced real love. I know what forgiveness is, even when I've done something so horrible."[12]

In February of 1998 she was put to death by lethal injection and went home to be with God. God's love transforms murderers into saints and changes hardened people into shining lights. It is scandalous because he loves us in an unconditional way, and he will meet us no matter where we are in life.

Though the thief on the cross suffered pain beyond belief, he also experienced the joy of his sins being lifted from his shoulders. He was free, paradoxically dying the most cruel and joyful death one can imagine. He had the promise of another life. The promise of forgiveness. The promise of a time when his pain would be no more.

The thief's encounter with Jesus reminds me of what John Piper calls "the solid logic of heaven."[13] This logic is found in Romans 8:32 where Paul writes that God "did not spare his own Son, but gave him up for us all—how will he not also, along with him, graciously give us all things?" Piper contends that on the surface this may seem like one of many promises of God, but its logic places it above the rest. Paul argues "from greater to lesser." This was a common mode of teaching. A teacher pointed to an extreme and said, "If this greater thing is true, then surely the lesser thing is true."

Romans 8:32 has both a foundation and a promise.[14] The foundation is that God "did not spare his own Son, but gave him up for us all." That is the greater thing, the amazing thing. Then the logic of heaven enters. Since he did not spare his own Son, "how will he not also, along with him, graciously give us all things?" That is the promise. Since God gave his own Son, the greater thing, God will provide for our needs, the lesser thing. Paul is saying that when the pressures of life are overwhelming and everything seems to be falling apart, look to the cross. Heaven's logic declares God's goodwill toward us in unquestionable and undeniable ways.

What does it mean to say God will "give us all things"? Part of the answer is found in the preceding verse, which says, "If God is for us, who can be against us?" (v. 31). This is the verse I end every service with at Central Christian Church in Vegas. God can take all of our heartache, hurt, and pain and bring good things out of it. We may still go through difficulty, but those difficulties, even death, don't conquer us because they do not conquer God. He will sustain us and bring good out of everything that happens to us. That is part of what's involved in the passionate love of God.

The M*A*S*H Church

One of my childhood memories is playing in the living room at night as my dad watched the hit television show *M*A*S*H*. It seemed like it was always on, and later I'd watch reruns of the show for years. The Mobile Army Surgical Hospital featured in the show was based on a real unit. It was the best known and most courageous of all the units, always on the edge of battle. Its members helped people whose bodies were crushed and broken. Without benefit of the best facilities or materials, they brought healing, love, and light to a dark place.

Years ago I heard a friend of mine give a talk on how spiritually we can learn a lot from *M*A*S*H*.[15] The church should function like a M*A*S*H unit—a place where broken people find healing, a trauma center for the world. He reminded me of all those characters on *M*A*S*H*. There was Father Mulcahy, the friendly, lovable priest. He was always available to listen to anyone, no matter who they were or what they had been through.

Then there was Radar. In many ways, he represented a broken person. He was timid and afraid. His character was based on a person who was born with an incomplete hand. This is why we often saw Radar carrying something to cover up his hand.

My favorite characters were Hawkeye and B. J., who were relentless toward anybody who acted arrogant or above the crowd. They would cut through people who were all talk and no action. Yet they maintained a sensitivity to those who were hurting.

And I had an adolescent crush on Margaret ("Hot Lips"), who went from one relationship to the next. Looking back now, she seems to me to represent a person who feels inadequate and because of that rushes out to people in all directions to fill her needs. Margaret would not expect the average church to welcome her.

Would Jesus welcome her? He welcomed Nicodemus, the woman at the well, Zacchaeus, the woman caught in adultery, and others. He did not drive them away; surely he would welcome Margaret. In fact, as he was dying, he welcomed a thief crucified next to him. He reached out in love to this broken outcast and set an example for us to be a spiritual M*A*S*H unit to the world.

So several years ago we started looking around as a church community in Las Vegas and asked, "Who is hurting that we can help, and who is not being reached?" That led to some new things for us.

We started reaching out relationally into the arts and entertainment arenas of Las Vegas, because nobody was really doing that. We realized that although our church had been in Las Vegas, one of the addiction hot spots of America, for decades, we had no drug, alcohol, or gambling recovery ministries. So we launched a recovery ministry that has grown to be the largest in the state. Our women began reaching out to strippers and those in adult entertainment with a message of love.

We began to look at some of our local prisons. In one of our women's prisons the most that had ever come to a religious event, according to the chaplain, was no more than a handful of women. So we prayed and researched and learned that a huge problem within the prison system centered on drug and alcohol recovery. We went into the prison offering a twelve-step recovery program and earned the right to eventually launch an extension campus of Central inside the prison in partnership with a nonprofit called God Behind Bars. With an on-site team, the worship and teaching are video from our weekend services.

Originally some women attended service to use it as an opportunity to be with their girlfriends. But over time, their hearts began to change. Slowly there was less making out and more hands lifted in worship. Today, almost half of the entire prison population at that women's prison attends church every weekend, filling every seat they will allow us to fill. The warden is supporting us and doors are opening across more and more prisons; a prison guard recently said that the prison church campus is actually changing the entire climate of the prison. Now the program has expanded into multiple states. But it all started when we asked, "Who is hurting and who is not being reached? How can we be a spiritual M*A*S*H unit to the world?"

Any time you start asking these questions, it will lead to challenges. Of course it is easy to talk about reaching the broken, but you have to know it is messy and there is a cost. We say it doesn't matter what you wear to church, we're just glad you came. But when a girl walks in wearing her Hooters outfit because she just got off work, are you truly going to practice what you preach? When a former key leader tells me he no longer wants his kids in the children's ministry with the type of kids that are there, what do you do? We've chosen to follow God in our context to help those who are broken find healing in Jesus. I know there are unique dynamics in Vegas, and I would never prescribe what we've done to another context, but the bottom line is in every city there are hurting people who are up and in and down and out, and they all need grace. They've hugged the cactus long enough.

Caring for the HIV Positive

Juan Carlos Ortiz is world famous for his global teaching ministry and his book *Disciple*. But what impresses me most about him is his unconditional love for his children. He tells of struggling with one teenage son. At age fifteen his son began to completely disregard his parents and his curfew. Juan Carlos and his wife lay awake many nights worrying about him. They disciplined him and argued with him. Household tension grew.

Finally, Ortiz decided to change the atmosphere. He said,

> I communicated to him that we would not rebuke him any longer. When he came in late the next evening, I went to his bedroom, hugged him, kissed him, and told him: "Do not take this hug and kiss as an approval of your conduct. I hugged and kissed you good night because I love you very dearly, not because I approve of what you do." After a few minutes he came to my bedroom, hugged and kissed me, and said: "Dad, do not take my hug and kiss as if I repented and will not come home late any more. I will keep on coming home late, but I love you because you are a great Dad." The lesson is that though the problem was not solved at that time, we were able to have a friendly relationship with our teenage son.[16]

At age eighteen, their son wrote an emotional letter informing them he was gay. The letter was not proud or jubilant, but filled with turmoil and sadness. He wrote, "I am leaving to save you troubles" and mentioned departing to another country. Though the Ortiz family felt cut to the heart, they decided to stand with their son, though they did not approve of his choices. They felt he should continue to live with them.

Juan Carlos Ortiz met with his ministry board and explained the situation. He acknowledged that he was prepared to resign and leave if the board thought that was appropriate, but the board concluded, "We are responsible *to* our children, not *for* our children. Each person is responsible for himself before God." Though the Ortizs' son knew of his parents' sadness, he also knew they would always love him.

At times people would call Ortiz's attention to the fact that his son was openly gay. Ortiz responded: "I know, but he is my son and I love him." No limit could be placed on their love.

Eventually, his son's medical tests revealed that he was HIV positive. Juan Carlos and his wife surrounded him with love. The shock of AIDS changed his life. He drew close to God and was baptized. He again became the joy of the house. He shared his faith with everybody and began playing piano again for God.

His final months were his most wonderful. He told his family not to be sad, because he was going to be with Jesus. "You will also die," he reminded them, "everybody will die after all. I will be better there than here. I will not have all these temptations, and I will be waiting for you."

Juan Carlos said, "My son taught me how to die."[17]

After his death the funeral was a testimony to everyone. Later the family was able to comfort some of his friends before they died, and one of his friends became a born-again Christian before passing away.

Juan Carlos Ortiz exemplifies the love of a parent, a love that reaches out despite unloveliness and loves in a radically transforming way. That is the kind of love the cross screams to us. It is God throwing his arms open, poised and ready to wrap them around his children and affirm his love. One church father asked, "How deep and high and wide is God's love?" He answered that it is as deep as the cross, which goes down even to the center of the earth. And it is as high as the heavens, and it spreads out across the east and the west declaring God's love to the world. God's love is deeper, wider, and higher than any unloveliness in our lives.

God's love is deeper than your deepest scars; heal through it. No matter how deep your scars are, Jesus proved God's love runs deeper when he chose the nails. He is the great wounded healer. Your wounds may be sensitive, your faith fragile, your sense of trust devastated, but think of Jesus on Calvary and remember his love is truly greater than anything we can comprehend. Discover healing in that love.

God's love is wider than your past; rejoice in it. The thief on the cross came from a rocky past, but Jesus extended his love anyway. God's love cancels your past. As the psalmist says, "For as high as the heavens are above the earth, so great is his love for those who fear him; as far as the east is from the west, so far has he removed our transgressions from us" (Ps. 103:11–12). You can travel to absolute north or south, but there is no absolute east or west. God's love has removed your sins without limit!

God's love is higher than your future; bank on it. Paul prayed that you "may have power, together with all the saints, to grasp how wide and long and high and deep is the love of Christ, and to know this love that surpasses knowledge—that you may be filled to the measure of all the fullness of God" (Eph. 3:18–19).

God's love is so profound it surpasses knowledge. His love goes before us into the future. We do not have to be afraid. We are not alone. His love carries us over rugged terrain and difficult times. We can bank on a future filled with love and goodness beyond anything we ever imagined! If God went to the extreme of the cross to save us, what kinds of extremes will he go to in allowing us to celebrate his goodness for eternity? We must open our hearts to his love and share it as part of the spiritual M*A*S*H unit to the world.

QUESTIONS FOR DISCUSSION

1. Do you have a favorite character or memory about the television show *M*A*S*H*?
2. In what ways should the church function like a M*A*S*H unit?
3. What does the cross teach us about the value of others?
4. Discuss the statement: "Without the cross we would be tempted to see evil in the world and believe God does not love us. But there stands the cross. I may not understand fully why suffering and evil pervade our world, but I can look to the cross and find comfort in God's response."
5. Read Romans 8:32. What makes this promise unique? In what area of your life do you need to claim this promise?

7

the wow factor

Life should not be a journey to the grave with the intention of arriving safely in a pretty and well preserved body, but rather to skid in broadside in a cloud of smoke, thoroughly used up, totally worn out, and loudly proclaiming "Wow! What a Ride!"

Hunter S. Thompson

As a toddler, my son went through a period where he asked me the same question countless times a day. A spider would be walking across the floor. "Dad," he'd say, "look at the spider! Is that *amazing*?" He was trying to make a statement, but he inflected it as a question. "Dad, do you see that cloud? Is that *amazing*?" The first couple times it was too cute, and my wife and I couldn't wait to tell our parents how remarkable their grandson was.

But then it went on . . . and on . . . and on. This phenomenon, where someone (especially young children learning language) repeat the same word or phrase over and over again, is called "perseveration." Only I wasn't sure that my wife and I could persevere through our son's constant amazement. We got this every day for months. "Dad, watch me run! Was I fast? Is that *amazing?*"

At this age, he sometimes still came into our room at night and climbed into bed with us. Half the time we were too wiped out to carry him back to his own bed. He was a wild sleeper, so I'd get kicked in the head and elbowed or would wake up with a finger up my nose. One morning after a particularly rough night of sleeping restlessly, he woke up and said, "Dad, I slept good. Is that *amazing?*" I thought, *I didn't! And it's not very* amazing!

My son challenged me without knowing it to start thinking about God differently. He lifted me from discouragement. Sleep *is* amazing (which every new parent learns to appreciate the hard way!). Spiders are amazing. Clouds are amazing. Life is amazing. And God, the author of amazement, is the creator of them all. He can breathe life into us when we are weary and worn and feeling discouraged.

Discouraged Followers

You may describe your life with a lot of words, but *amazing* isn't one of them. Maybe you're married with kids. You seek to raise your family well, but lately things seem to be coming unglued. Your marriage looks healthy, although below the surface lies a quiet despair. You spend little quality time with your spouse. Communication has broken down, and evenings are filled with a million details to get the kids ready for the next day. The laundry and dirty dishes are piled high. You look at the busyness of your life and fight the temptation to just feel overwhelmed; in a word, you're discouraged.

Or maybe you're single, and you work hard and play hard. In a group you are the life of the party, but in private you wrestle with loneliness and the future. Perhaps you long for a mate, someone who will last longer than a few dates, or maybe you love being single, but you haven't felt close to God for longer than you want to admit. You think, *In high school, this is not how I envisioned my life. Is this what it's all about? Is there nothing more?* You're discouraged by your lack of progress.

Discouragement is like a cold, blustery wind that freezes everything it touches. It dampens enthusiasm, erases smiles, and leaves loved ones bent over like a flower with no sun. It enters our lives at many levels and in different ways. One critical comment can bring discouragement for months. A broken dream can drain hope from our hearts. Uncontrollable circumstances can beat us down until we're ready to quit.

On the first Easter Sunday, Jesus met two discouraged disciples trekking down the dusty road from Jerusalem to Emmaus—a small village seven miles from Jerusalem. There was no spring in their step, no joy in their countenance. On Friday the Roman authorities handed Jesus over to be whipped and beaten. They crucified and buried him. Darkness covered the earth. Despair and hopelessness prevailed. Their hearts were filled with a deep inner ache, the kind of gaping hole that comes from grieving a loved one's death.

These men walked and conversed. Their mouths moved rapidly as they replayed the past week's events. Palm Sunday seemed like years ago, though it had only been a week since Jesus rode victoriously into Jerusalem. So much had occurred since then. Christ was crucified. Their friends, the disciples of Jesus, retreated in fear. Jesus' inner circle struggled to make sense of it all as the crushing weight of Friday loomed over everything.

As these two walked, "Jesus himself came up and walked along with them; but they were kept from recognizing him" (Luke 24:15–16). The Emmaus travelers perceived this stranger was not "in the know." One named Cleopas was amazed that this man had not heard about Jesus of Nazareth; he asked,

> Are you only a visitor to Jerusalem and do not know the things that have happened? . . . He was a prophet, powerful in word and deed before God and all the people. The chief priests and our rulers handed him over to be sentenced to death, and they crucified him; but we had hoped that he was the one who was going to redeem Israel. And what is more, it is the third day since all this took place. (Luke 24:18–21)

Jews believed that the deceased hovered over their bodies for three days before they were gone. Now the third day had come and Jesus was totally gone. The two relayed to the stranger that some of the women had gone to the tomb but found no body. To make things worse, the women claimed to have seen angelic visions announcing Jesus' resurrection! They poured out the whole unlikely story of a resurrection. These guys felt frustrated, bewildered, and tired. The concept of resurrection seemed like pie in the sky.

Love That Doesn't Die

Those who discovered the empty tomb on Easter morning were amazed, terrified, and confused. The religious leaders didn't know what to make of the empty tomb. They created a plan; they gave the soldiers a large sum of money and told them, "You are to say, 'His disciples came during the night

124

and stole him away while we were asleep'" (Matt. 28:13). They blamed the empty tomb on grave robbers.

Mary Magdalene also blamed the empty tomb on grave robbers. When she first arrived at the tomb early in the morning, she found no body. To Peter she exclaimed, "They have taken the Lord out of the tomb, and we don't know where they have put him!" (John 20:2). As she stood at the grave, weeping, Jesus called her by name. She recognized the true resurrected Jesus. Overwhelmed with joy, she hurried off to tell the disciples, "I have seen the Lord!" (v. 18).

These men on the road to Emmaus had their doubts that Jesus had risen from the dead. Rather than comforting them with soothing words, Jesus rebuked them for their ignorance of God's Word. He showed them all the places where the Old Testament described the suffering that Jesus would endure. Still unsure about this stranger, they wanted to hear more.

Many of us walk Emmaus roads, oblivious to Jesus' presence. We trudge along unaware that he's walking beside us to bring us encouragement. Maybe our heart weighs heavy with the burden of a child who is living far from God. Maybe the weight of our own failures slumps us over. The stock market may keep our stomach in knots. A sense of inadequacy may force a limp.

In the midst of their despair that day, the disciples on the road to Emmaus found themselves accompanied by Jesus. Arriving at their destination, they convinced him to stay over. At dinner Jesus took bread and broke it. The act seemed so characteristic and familiar that "their eyes were opened and they recognized him, and he disappeared from their sight" (Luke 24:31). The image of his broken body and shed blood became the very thing that opened their eyes. In that moment, everything changed!

I envision these men shouting and dancing for joy. Maybe Jesus' face looked more exhilarated at revealing himself. God's power specializes in helping the helpless, in reaching out to the hurting, in bringing encouragement to desperate situations. Encouragement had walked along beside them the entire time. They just needed the spiritual eyes to see it.

They immediately sprinted the seven miles back to Jerusalem. They found Jesus' disciples in their secret location and said, "It is true! The Lord has risen and has appeared to Simon" (v. 34).

The disciples were overwhelmed with joy, relief, and gratitude. If Jesus rose from the dead, then his teaching held true, God's love remained available, and their future looked entirely different. Life conquered death and prevailed over evil.

And it still does. Because Jesus rose from the dead, there is hope for our children, hope for our marriage, and hope for our situation. There is love for the difficult times, joy in the most unlikely times, and companionship at all times. Jesus' resurrection screams that we are not alone. The hope of Sunday conquers the despair of Friday.

Power for Unlikely Places

Paul writes that the same power God "exerted in Christ when he raised him from the dead and seated him at his right hand in the heavenly realms" is available to us today (Eph. 1:20). God's power is "for us," literally *toward* us (v. 19). If someone's heart is toward you, they actively desire to help you; they want to do good for you. God desires for us to experience his power in life. Paul shares three ways that God publicly declared his power: (1) he raised Jesus from the dead, (2) he placed him at God's right hand, and (3) he placed all things under him. He did all that for us! Theodoret, the ancient theologian and bishop, once said, "To know the power of his resurrection is to know the purpose of the resurrection."[1] God's purpose was to bring all things under Christ, including us.

When I am discouraged and frustrated, I remember that Jesus' resurrection revealed power in the most unlikely place—a graveyard. His resurrection can also bring power and love to another unlikely place—my heart. When I'm worn out as a parent, he brings encouragement. When I'm against a wall at work, he brings strength. When I'm grieving a loved one's death, he instills peace. He is the only one who can make every day Sunday. But there's a catch—I must have faith in Jesus' resurrection power for my life. Without this faith I am left in a graveyard of despair. Søren Kierkegaard said, "Have you considered what it is to despair? Alas, it is to deny that God is love! Think that over properly, one who despairs abandons himself (yes, so you think); nay, he abandons God!"[2]

We don't have to despair. Jesus walks beside us, and if we will only believe and walk in faith, he will allow us to experience amazing love. He specializes in rescuing people from personal graveyards.

In my teenage years I struggled in the graveyard of drug addiction. For years I used drugs daily. God's grace to me in that time still amazes me. I've also walked in the graveyard of ignorance. I entered college with few skills due to partying in high school. I never took the ACT or SAT; I knew if I did I'd fail spectacularly.

The school let me in provisionally, assuming I'd take the tests in a couple weeks, but I conveniently missed them again and again. When I turned in my first English essay, my professor had a look of shock on her face. The essay was several pages long with terrible punctuation, no paragraphs, and loads of run-on sentences. My years of addiction had crippled my learning. I realized I would not make it another day in college if I did not get a grip.

When my friends went out on the weekends, I went to the library and pored over English grammar books. With the help of many wonderful teachers, I learned how to write and type correctly. I faced many discouraging months and struggled with tremendous feelings of inadequacy, but I pulled through because I had people around me who cared. I regularly hit my knees and cried out to God for the strength, patience, and ability to learn. He poured courage into my empty heart.

Miracles in a Graveyard

What is your personal graveyard? Your relationship with your children may resemble a tombstone—hard, rough, heavy. You've tried to be a good parent, but distrust and frustration have taken over. Does it seem like an unlikely place for a miracle? So did the tombstone outside Jerusalem.

Your job may frustrate you to no end—the same boring tasks over and over again, the same challenges and obstacles. Jesus specializes in rolling tombstones away. He can walk into your graveyard and bring resurrection, light, and a future.

Your marriage may feel like a graveyard—cold words, cold looks, and colder isolation. The future of your relationship may seem grim. Your marriage may seem like the most unlikely place for hope to invade. So did the graveyard outside Jerusalem.

Tony and Charlotte found themselves in a marital graveyard. Tony had hurt his back working as an electrician and required multiple back surgeries for numerous disc problems. Each time it appeared the problem was fixed, but each time his pain came back. The pain, along with feelings of inadequacy at not being able to work, led Tony into a deep depression.

Charlotte began to harbor resentment because her needs were going unmet. After two and a half years of Tony's chronic pain, the pressure seemed too much. She said, "We were both so wrapped up in our own pity that we failed to see what we were doing to each other. The only thing that kept us together was the fact that we couldn't afford to get a divorce. So we waited patiently until Tony could get back to work so that we could ironically get our lives back in order without each other."[3] Their relationship felt cold and hard. Tony found solace with friends in Narcotics Anonymous and Charlotte poured her life into their kids.

With divorce looming, they decided to bring their kids to church. They wanted to help build them spiritually since they knew the divorce would be hard on them. At the time, it never dawned on them that God wanted to perform a miracle in the two of them, not just their children. As they tried to navigate their relational graveyard, they began to experience the resurrection power of Christ through their children and church. Weeks passed as they saved money to get the divorce. They sensed God calling them to surrender to him and to give him complete control of their marriage.

Tony says, "The more vertical we grew, the more horizontal we grew. God's compass set our marriage on a course where we began to take care of each other's needs ahead of our own. The more we cherished and supported each other, the more we realized that we were still deeply in love."[4] They started talking and listening to each other and learning about each other again. As they reached out to God, he performed a miracle. That is what God specializes in doing.

"Give in to Christ and the miracles he can produce. Trust him to compel you to renew your marriage," counsels Charlotte. "Don't ask him to change your spouse, but to change you and make you into who you need to be to renew your marriage."⁵ Tony and Charlotte, like the travelers on the road to Emmaus, found that Jesus loves to bring victory to what seems like a bleak graveyard. He loves to bring wow moments into ordinary lives.

A Wow Life

Business consultant and futurist Tom Peters advocates the "Pursuit of Wow!" He claims individuals who succeed in the future will view life with a wow attitude. Wow involves experiencing life to its fullest. It is life at full throttle.

Christians, of all people, should live with a wow factor. Wow people live in light of the resurrection. Opening our eyes to God's fingerprints, we find ourselves saying "wow" regularly.

You pray for your marriage, asking God to change your heart, and you notice a real difference.

You renew your commitment to change for the better and ask God to help you get control of your habits. You begin to feel spiritually connected and infused with new motivation.

That quick card you sent to a friend was received during one of her most difficult times. The note brought new hope and encouraged her to keep going.

Jesus' resurrection allows us to draw on past resources to move into the future with faith and courage. We draw on spiritual resources beyond ourselves and realize that "I can do all things through Christ who strengthens me" (Phil. 4:13 NKJV). Wow lives are full of love even in the midst of pain, full of promise despite critics, and full of faith even in desperate circumstances.

Jennifer is living a wow life after coming through many personal graveyards. At age eleven, she discovered two things that eventually almost killed her: purging and alcohol. Initially, her worries in life seemed to vanish. She could eat and purge all week and get drunk on the weekends. This pattern continued for years, throughout middle school. She would be disciplined for getting drunk, but that never stopped her. When she was a freshman in high school, she came home one day to learn that her dad had moved out. Her mom blamed Jennifer for his leaving. She unleashed her rage on her, calling her evil, unwanted, hated by her father, and, her favorite phrase, "from the devil."

Jennifer says, "At that time I tried to reach up to God; I thought if he loved me, he would help me and make her stop. One Easter Sunday morning, which was my fifteenth birthday, my mom refused to take me to church with them, telling me I was too evil to go. I remember sobbing, 'God, why do you hate me so much?'"[6]

Lashing out, Jennifer downed 130 diet pills and a bottle of Motrin in front of her mom. What she remembers before she lost consciousness is her sister begging her reluctant mom to call the ambulance. When the ambulance arrived the attendants pumped her stomach, and she was admitted to lockdown for juvenile delinquency.

Six months after she returned home, she learned that her dad had remarried. The realization that he would never be coming back put her in a tailspin. She binged on alcohol and drugs and then checked herself into a psychiatric hospital where she remained for several months. She was only sixteen.

After her release she continued to get into trouble, running away from home seven times. Eventually the court issued her an ultimatum, and she entered military school. There she smoked heavily, talked like a sailor, and acted as tough as possible. Inside she was terrified, alone, and dying. In military school her drug use skyrocketed—acid, ecstasy, cocaine, and marijuana. She regularly mixed all her drugs together and used them until she passed out. She began dealing to support her habit, but soon she was using all the drugs she was supposed to be dealing. She was in trouble, in a graveyard of her own making.

As she walked this lonely road, she began to realize she did not have to walk it alone. Jennifer says, "I can't explain how hard it was for me to turn to a God who I believed hated me. He was the only chance I had to survive. The miracles unfolded. I went from a treatment center to a three-quarter house, to a halfway house, to sober houses. I realized I was a valuable human being. I was staying sober and dealing with anorexia; I weighed only ninety-one pounds. God provided all my needs as I started to heal."[7]

At twenty-one Jennifer started over with only three backpacks filled with clothes and eighty dollars to her name. But she started over aware of Jesus' presence. She slept on people's couches, borrowed a bicycle to ride to work and to AA meetings, and fell on her knees every day to thank God for life. She says, "I learned I was not responsible for the actions and behaviors of my parents. I also learned I was accountable for my choices despite my parents' behaviors. I realize Jesus Christ is and always was the higher power of recovery. And I have discovered the person God intended me to be."[8] She began living a wow life!

Jennifer is now in her thirties. She is a faithful servant in her church, active in recovery ministry, and is married to a wonderful Christian man. She has also been blessed with two beautiful kids. Eventually, she came to a place of forgiveness for her family. She says, "I love my mom, sister, and father very much. I pray God blesses them with the same joy and freedom I have. I harbor no resentment toward them. God has many unopened packages of miracles that each person can have, but you gotta ask."[9]

Jennifer discovered the power of the resurrection of Jesus. She encountered the love and healing that only he can bring. Do you need encouragement? Jesus offers spiritual resources for the journey of life. His victory is your victory! Your future may seem dark, but not as dark as the sky at Jesus' death. Your resources may appear empty, but not as empty as Jesus' were when he carried the cross to Calvary.

Like those travelers on the road to Emmaus, you can find great encouragement in the victory Jesus has already won! When you hear the alarm go off Monday morning, remember Sunday. As the angels proclaimed on Easter, "He is not here; he has risen!" (Luke 24:6). Let him rise in your heart. Allow him to bring life to your personal graveyard.

QUESTIONS FOR DISCUSSION

1. What discourages people?
2. Share a time when you sensed God rescued you from a "personal graveyard."
3. Read Ephesians 1:18–20. Discuss the kind of power Paul says is available to us.
4. How do we access God's power?
5. How does the resurrection bring encouragement to your life?
6. Brainstorm practical ways you and your church can encourage others in your community.

8

a little crazy for God

When the whole world is crazy, it doesn't pay to be sane.

Terry Goodkind

Raising kids in Vegas sometimes feels a little crazy. Recently we were riding in our gray minivan with our two kids. We came up to a stop sign and before us was a billboard for a radio station that said, "The Hits Are Back." The picture on the billboard showed six women with no tops on. They had their backs turned and showed their backsides in G-strings. My son, who was seven, looked over at his sister and innocently asked, "Emma, which naked girl is your favorite? My favorite is the one with brown hair."

All the air was sucked out of the minivan as my wife and I gasped. Then in a moment of pure parenting brilliance my wife turned around and said, "Ethan, we don't have favorite naked girls!" I'm thinking, *No, just naked girls!* Only in Vegas.

By now you may be saying to yourself, "I'm glad I don't live in Las Vegas." But we love it here because God has called us here. We aren't simply living in Las Vegas, we're on the mission field of Las Vegas. And wherever we live, whatever our career path is, we can all take part in God's purpose for our lives, even if it feels a little crazy.

In fact, discovering our unique purpose and gifts, and leveraging them to help others, is one of the most important paths to fulfillment. Often the emptiness and restlessness we feel are directly connected to this area of our lives. Emptiness results from making life all about me and my needs as opposed to God and others. Of course my needs are important as well, but in serving others I meet one of my most fundamental needs to live beyond myself.

One man who discovered that God's purpose was wide open to him no matter what he had done was Saul. He was born in Tarsus, in modern-day Turkey, two millennia ago. Though a Roman citizen he was a Jew, schooled in Jerusalem. He studied under Gamaliel, a leading religious teacher of his day. Saul was very intelligent; he climbed the ladder quickly and reached the upper echelons of religious leadership for the Jewish people: he was a Pharisee who sat on the Jewish ruling council.

He took it upon himself to try to snuff out Christianity. Being trained in law, he chose to go through the proper legal channel—the Jewish high priest. He petitioned for and received blank arrest warrants to arrest Christians. Saul yanked Christians out of their homes, locked them up, and threw the book at them. He separated fathers from children, wives from husbands, and friends from loved ones.

One day as he was walking on the road to Damascus, a light suddenly shone around him. A voice from heaven said, "Saul, Saul, why do you persecute me?"

"Who are you, Lord?" asked Saul. Then he heard the words he never thought he'd hear in a million years.

The voice said, "I am Jesus, whom you are persecuting." All his preconceptions and presuppositions melted before him. Jesus, the Messiah? He would never recover from that moment.

He stood up, but his heart remained floored. His eyes were blinded, and he could not see. His friends led him to a house on Straight Street. For three days, Saul prayed and fasted. He was in the locker room of defeat. He realized he had run the ball the wrong way, opposing Jesus, the very Son of God.

God came to Ananias and sent him to where Saul was staying. Ananias walked in and told Saul that he had been sent by God to minister to him. He told him in essence, "The game is only half over. You are not finished. God has great things in store for you." As he ministered to him, "Immediately, something like scales fell from Saul's eyes, and he could see again" (Acts 9:18). For the first time, he was able to see—not just in a physical sense but in a spiritual sense as well.

That encounter with Jesus changed his life. Saul (later called Paul) got up and was baptized. He became a follower of Jesus Christ and would go on to become a great missionary and one of the greatest minds in Christianity. He wrote many of the letters in the New Testament. He discovered purpose beyond his failure and became a spiritual surgeon ministering to others.

We have seen Jesus' love meet people mired in meaninglessness, loneliness, guilt, success, pain, insignificance, and discouragement. He has healed and helped many of us, but Jesus does not expect this to be the end of the story. Our healing is completed as we discover our own gifts and get involved helping others. We go from being helped to helping, from being changed to assisting others in change, and from being loved to loving. We may still be wounded, but now we are wounded healers. God wants to use us in our broken places.

Perspective Shift

One benefit of having the "scales fall from our eyes" in a spiritual sense is that it affects how we see others. Naturally, we want to put people in certain boxes. A guy or girl walks in, and we see what they are wearing and frame them up. We make decisions based on their skin tone, their makeup quality, their shoes, and their car. In mere moments we label and categorize.

Paul speaks of how our new identity starts with how we see Jesus, then affects both how we see ourselves and how we see others: "So we have stopped evaluating others from a human point of view," he wrote. "At one time we thought of Christ merely from a human point of view. How differently we know him now! This means that anyone who belongs to Christ has become a new person. The old life is gone; a new life has begun!" (2 Cor. 5:16–17 NLT).

Notice that Paul's view of Jesus is what changed. We don't just see him from a human standpoint anymore: a Jewish guy who taught people to love others, wore a toga-looking thing, and had long hair. We realize by faith that he is the Savior of the world, God incarnate who has come to earth. This perspective shift affects everything. We don't see Jesus merely from a human standpoint and we don't see others or ourselves from a purely human standpoint either.

Yet getting around our stereotypes is quite a challenge, as *The Washington Post* discovered when they did a study on context and how people see others in different situations. They reached out to Joshua Bell to see if he'd help them with an experiment.

Many would say that Bell is the most celebrated classical violin player in America. He sells out many different classical venues where people hold back their urge to clear their throat until the appropriate time out of respect for the music. Bell is a violin master.

The Washington Post asked Bell to take his violin and go down to the metro train station in Washington, DC, and randomly start playing. They wanted to see what would happen. Would people recognize the best classical music the world has to offer? Would people see a brilliant musician who is playing there? Would anyone even notice?

Bell wasn't going to show up and whip out some violin he got at the thrift store. His violin is a Stradivarius made in the 1700s. It has never been refurbished and it is worth over 3.5 million dollars. They set up video cameras to capture the scene, and he took out his Stradivarius and started playing beautiful classical music.

The Washington Post was initially concerned that a mob might break out, yet in reality hardly anyone noticed. He played for about forty minutes and over a thousand people walked by him without noticing. Why? Because he played in the context of a guy standing in a train station making music on an old violin. They immediately just saw a street musician, or even a bum.

At the end of his forty minutes he had collected $32.17 in tips in his violin case—a case that was likely worth a small fortune itself! One lady actually recognized him and the look on her face said, "Oh my gosh. You are Joshua Bell!" What kind of bizarre moment must that have been for her? I guess she thought things were going really hard for him, so she dropped in $20. This was an amazing study, which proved that people tend to have a hard time seeing outside of certain contexts.

As Christians we must never see someone apart from the gospel and God's grace. Our culture may see a businessman who has done well as a snob who would never need community and must be selfish to have "made it," but we see that God loves him and that he needs to be loved. Our culture may see a homeless person as without value to society, but we see that God provided salvation to give this homeless person a home that will not perish. Our culture may see a beautiful woman as having it all together and not needing affirmation, but we see a woman who needs to be encouraged and is searching for hope. Our culture may see a criminal who does not deserve any blessings in life, but we see that Jesus loves the criminal so much that he died to break his bondage to sin. We must not value people based on what they do, but on who they are—or could be—in Christ.

Making Change

Paul's story is radical, but it may not be our story. We read about Paul's encounter, this amazing, dramatic thing— light shining from heaven, the voice of God speaking—and it's easy to start to feel like second-class citizens in God's kingdom.

For most people there is no flash of light, no three days without food or water, no scales falling from our eyes. That is okay. The issue is not *how* or *when* we were converted. The issue is *what* our Christian experience is like *now*. The journey remains more important than the onetime experience.

Encounters with Jesus' love challenge us to serve. Paul could have simply been baptized and gone back to building a nice cozy retirement package. But his baptism served as a launching place to a lifetime of service. Paul later wrote,

> Now about spiritual gifts, brothers, I do not want you to be ignorant. . . . There are different kinds of gifts, but the same Spirit. There are different kinds of service, but the same Lord. There are different kinds of working, but the same God works all of them in all men. Now to each one the manifestation of the Spirit is given for the common good. (1 Cor. 12:1, 4–7)

All of us are given abilities and gifts, and Paul emphasizes that we are not to be ignorant of this. At least twenty different gifts are mentioned in the New Testament, and there are likely more. God created us so that we are unlike anybody else. In the discovery and use of our spiritual gifts, we realize our uniqueness. We must use our gifts to share the love of God with others. If we don't use our unique gifts, there will be broken hearts that will never be healed, confused minds that will never be given clarity, and souls that will not experience forgiveness.

Certain gifts operate behind the scenes—compassion, mercy, hospitality. Some are more up-front—teaching, preaching. Some are supernatural—healing, prophecy. Some gifts we receive from the Holy Spirit we didn't possess before we became Christians. Or maybe we already possessed certain gifts and God's Spirit empowers us to use them powerfully for his kingdom. God takes our natural gifts and enhances them even more; he uses them to minister to other people.

Thousands who have encountered Jesus have accepted the challenge, just like Paul, to serve him daily. They get the job done wherever he sends them. We won't hear about them on CNN or read about them in *Time* or *Newsweek*, but this coming week hundreds of thousands of them will share Jesus' love. They will do pro bono legal work for the poor, build homes for the needy, volunteer at soup kitchens, and give sandwiches over a food line in our inner cities. They'll wash the sheets from their church's nursery, stuff envelopes, and help anyone who has a need. Some will load a food truck in Africa and take it to a group of people in need; they'll teach poverty-stricken farmers how to develop their crops so they can fight famine. Through small and large acts of kindness, they change the world.

I'm moved by the story that Bill Wilson tells about his life (a different Bill than the founder of Alcoholics Anonymous). He was walking with his mom in St. Petersburg, Florida, at the age of fourteen. He remembered his mom was tired. She had a hard day and wasn't saying much. They came to a particular street corner not far from where she served as a bartender. His mom looked at him and said, "Son, I can't do this anymore. I need you to stay right here and wait for me." Then she left.

Bill stayed there the rest of the day and through the night. For three full days he waited on that street corner for his mom to come back. Can you imagine the fear and anxiety of a kid standing on the corner for that long? During this time a man noticed him as he walked by daily on his way to work and back. One day he said to Bill, "What are you doing here? I've seen you here the last couple days; what's going on?"

Bill said, "My mom told me to wait here for her. She's going to come back." The man told him that at least he had to eat and brought him some food. The next day he walked by and Bill was still standing there. He said, "Look, why don't you come and stay with me? I'll take care of you. We'll keep watching for your mom. Maybe something happened? We'll find out what went on."

Bill's mom never came back, and the man ended up taking Bill in. He was a follower of Jesus and he took Bill to a Sunday school retreat where he surrendered his life to Jesus.

God used a horrible experience to bring good to Bill's life. He showed Bill how to trust in his faithfulness when everyone else lets us down.

Do you know what Bill did with that experience? As an adult he went to Brooklyn, New York, to one of the worst sections of America. This is a place where the streets are filled with crack vials and drug syringes, where prostitution is through the roof and kids are subject to all kinds of abuse. Bill started a Sunday school to reach out to kids who had been left and abandoned and didn't have anything, kids who were just like he was at fourteen. Today he leads Metro Ministries and runs the largest Sunday school in the United States with over 22,000 children every week.

Utilizing over fifty buses and thirty vans, they bring kids into a huge warehouse where they do a full-blown Sunday school program. For many of these kids it's the only time they hear a message of hope, get life skills, and are encouraged to stay in school and stay away from drugs. Bill uses his gifts and his unique experiences to impact the lives of thousands. He refused to become a victim and make excuses.

Go for It

We are masters of excuses, aren't we?

"I'm not good enough for God to use."
"With a past like mine, God could never use me."
"God has ministers and pastors to do that sort of thing."
"When I get control of a certain area of my life, then I'll use my talents for him."

We overlook the motley crew that God used throughout the Bible. The people he empowered were ordinary, sometimes crooked, and often deeply flawed. They were miles from perfect. In fact, many of them would make the hall of mess-ups. But God used them to make profound changes in the world.

The apostle Paul went on to do amazing things, but he wasn't flawless. One particular weakness plagued him so much he pled with God to take it away, but God responded, "'My grace is sufficient for you, for my power is made per-fect in weakness.' Therefore," Paul said, "I will boast all the more gladly about my weaknesses, so that Christ's power may rest on me" (2 Cor. 12:9). God's power is made perfect in weakness. It's so easy to feel inadequate—but God doesn't want what we can *do*; he wants *us*. He can then use us for a greater purpose.

How can you discover your gifts? You can take a spiritual gifts survey or personality test. You can ask people around you for wisdom. But the best way to discover your gifts is to get out there and try a few things. Don't wait for the light to turn green before you do something; assume the light *is* green unless God stops you with a red one.

What is your dream for God? Go for it. Billy Graham had a dream to share Jesus' love through preaching. Since there was nobody to preach to, he preached to the trees. One day he sensed God telling him those trees would soon be people. Your gift may not be preaching, but encouragement, mercy, faith, or prayer. The important thing is that you *do* something, even if it feels a little crazy.

In one of my favorite passages Paul said, "If it seems we are crazy, it is to bring glory to God. And if we are in our right minds, it is for your benefit" (2 Cor. 5:13 NLT). The context in this verse is that Festus, a member of the ruling class, had levied a charge against Paul that he was out of his mind because of the way he was acting. Paul is referencing a literal charge of being crazy.

Anybody called you crazy lately? If so, you are in good company! If you aren't getting criticized for something it may be because you aren't doing *anything*.

Here are a few things we've done recently that seemed out there for us. When we first went into the prisons with church campuses in Las Vegas, it felt a little crazy. The first time my wife and I invited an adult dancer and her husband into our small group, and they showed up at our home, it felt a little crazy. When we were in the midst of a financial meltdown in Vegas and our church was severely resource challenged, we dedicated a significant amount of money to give away to the hurting outside our community, and that felt crazy. When my wife picked one of our kids up from the kids' area at church and heard a four-year-old kid yell across the classroom words he's heard at home: "Someone get off their a— and bring me a f—ing beer!" it felt a little crazy, but we were so glad that family was in church!

Recently, a guy left our church after services and told a volunteer on his way out, "I think a man in the bleachers just died. You might want to check it out." What? We go up to check, and a man is sprawled over the seats in front of him and he isn't moving. Thankfully, he wasn't dead, but smashed drunk. He must have gotten so much of the message that when he stood up at the end of the service he passed out cold. And the most bizarre thing is the other person didn't even check to see if he was okay; he just let someone know on his way out! And that definitely feels a little crazy, but we can't get so comfortable as believers that we stop doing crazy stuff for God.

When you help people who don't deserve a second chance with a third, fourth, and fifth chance, people will say you're crazy—I call it being a Christian! When we commit to pray for someone we hardly know every day because we feel led to do it, people will say you're crazy. When you start going after your dream for God and people think you are nuts, keep going. They accused Paul of being crazy too.

And remember that your crazy and my crazy aren't the same thing. Don't go out and do what I did; get together with some friends and dream and plan and play and take some risks for *you*. Don't make your crazy step of faith for God mandatory for all other believers, and don't judge everyone else's risk of faith! When somebody steps out in faith and fails, it is easy to think what they did was just crazy in a dumb way. Yet when it works, we call them brilliant! The truth is most of us have more failures than successes.

What would it look like for you to get a little crazy for God this year? To stretch your personal faith? To take a risk for you, even if it doesn't seem risky to others? To begin to exercise your unique gifts and experiences? When we are touched by Jesus' love we can share that with others, irrespective of the cost. And we'll discover the satisfaction that results from living in our purpose.

QUESTIONS FOR DISCUSSION

1. Have you ever felt like a second-class citizen in God's kingdom because your testimony is not a dramatic story of someone saved from skid row?
2. Read 1 Corinthians 12:1–11. Discuss some of the spiritual gifts mentioned there.
3. Discuss the statement: "The best way to discover my gifts is to get out there and try some things. Too often we wait for the light to turn green before we do something.

Assume the light *is* green unless God stops you with a red one. What is your dream for God? Go for it."

4. What is your spiritual gift? What are some practical steps you can take to discover your gifts?

5. What are some practical ways you can use your gifts to share God's love with others?

conclusion

ENOUGH FOR ME

We must be emptied of that which fills us, so that we may be filled with that of which we are empty.

St. Augustine

Brennan Manning's memoir *All Is Grace* is a moving read about a broken person who has taught me so much about God's love in his writing. Many know Brennan's story. He's a great writer on the theme of grace who became well-known for his book *The Ragamuffin Gospel*.

Brennan is in his late 70s now. The crowds that packed out his speaking tours have long gone. He has to have someone help him get up, help him eat, and help him do even the most basic functions of life. He's alone except for his caretaker many days. He's developed "wet-brain" from his struggle with alcoholism, a medical condition that affects his memory, among other things. Reading his memoir felt like a good-bye, and reminded me how much I owe him.

I only met him once. I didn't know much about him at the time, but a friend invited me to a breakfast he was hosting at a church. Nobody else showed! It was just my friend and I, the pastor of the church, and Brennan.

This sort of embarrassing moment became a remarkable gift. He sat with us all morning and shared his story of his time as a priest, his alcoholism, his marriage, and through it all the power of God's grace. I remember that we met until almost lunchtime, and then he headed to a local Alcoholics Anonymous meeting that was happening in town. He had such presence and such compassion. After this meeting I was so moved by this humble man I devoured most of his books.

Alcoholism continued to hound him through his life and ministry. In *The Ragamuffin Gospel* he shared a question and response that have been quoted many times. He wrote,

> Often I have been asked, "Brennan, how is it possible that you became an alcoholic after you got saved?" It is possible because I got battered and bruised by loneliness and failure; because I got discouraged, uncertain, guilt-ridden, and took my eyes off Jesus. Because the Christ-encounter did not change me into an angel.[1]

Even after writing this he succumbed to the bottle again and again, and ultimately it destroyed his marriage and much of his life. He movingly describes missing his mom's funeral because he blacked out at a nearby hotel from having too much to drink.

In his memoir he says he has a shorter answer to the question now: "'Brennan, how is it possible that you became an alcoholic after you got saved?' Answer: 'These things happen.'"[2]

Sadly, these things do happen. None of us are immune to temptation or the pull of sin; none of us are ever beyond the need of God's grace in Jesus. Life this side of heaven is messy, and people of faith can often find themselves living in a contradiction they can't explain. The temptation can be to pull away from God, but what I appreciated about Brennan's memoir is that he's still clinging to Jesus. He could define himself by a lot of things—failed priest, divorcé, alcoholic. But he's spending his final days hanging on to Jesus.

I'm not seeking to justify Brennan's life or overlook his mistakes. Sin is serious and needs to be faced with the grace and power of God. But his story reminds me that we can all be justified by Jesus. That no matter how many distractions of phony things we seek to fill our lives, he is the only one who is enough.

We've seen how Jesus' love impacted the lives of so many he met. Nicodemus sought him at night, undercover, and later he appeared to help bury Jesus. One woman met him midday at a well and led many in her hometown to Christ. Zacchaeus encountered him while perched in a sycamore-fig tree and gave half his money to the poor. An adulterous woman stood before him condemned and walked away free to sin no more. An ill woman touched his cloak after twelve years of suffering and her faith brought healing. A thief accompanied him to the cross and that day entered paradise. Two men unknowingly walked with him on the road to Emmaus and rediscovered purpose and meaning. Each of them encountered Jesus. Each of them experienced change.

Jesus longs to encounter us and lead us to a life filled with his blessing. He is the only one who can fill us when everything else leaves us empty. He wants to use us as wounded healers. He desires to deploy us to a hurting world to make a difference. No matter where we are today, Jesus welcomes us to experience more of his love and power, just like the characters he encountered centuries ago. His love will carry us the distance.

He's the only one worth hanging on to, no matter what sort of "these things happen" we find ourselves in.

notes

Chapter 1 Hunger Games

1. Alfred Edersheim, *The Life and Times of Jesus the Messiah: Complete and Unabridged in One Volume* (Peabody, MA: Hendrickson, 1993), 265.

2. Ibid.

3. Anne Lamott, *Traveling Mercies: Some Thoughts on Faith* (New York: Random House, 1999), 61.

4. "Barna Survey Examines Changes in Worldview of Christians over the Past 13 Years," http://www.barna.org/barna-update/article/21-transformation/252-barna-survey-examines-changes-in-worldview-among-christians-over-the-past-13-years.

5. Ibid.

6. Dallas Willard, *The Divine Conspiracy: Rediscovering Our Hidden Life in God* (New York: Harper Collins, 1998), 68.

7. Blaise Pascal, *The Mind on Fire: Anthology of the Writings of Blaise Pascal*, ed. James M. Houston (Sisters, OR: Multnomah, 1989), 166.

8. William Willimon, as quoted in *Leadership* 11, no. 4.

Chapter 2 All the Lonely People

1. Winona Ryder, quoted in *Plugged In* 6, no. 4 (April 2001): 16.

2. Douglas Coupland, quoted in J. Brent Bill, "Loneliness Virus: Douglas Coupland's World," *Christian Century* (November 8, 2000), www.findarticles.com/cf_0/m1058/31_1117/67328510/print.jhtml.

3. John Cacioppo, "Why Loneliness Is Bad for Your Health," *Jet* (Aug. 28, 2000), www.findarticles.com/cf_0/m1355/12u_98/64910137/print.jhtml.

4. Henri Nouwen, *Making All Things New: An Invitation to the Spiritual Life* (San Francisco: Harper & Row, 1981), 51–53.

5. Mark Moore, *The Chronological Life of Christ Volume 1: From Glory to Galilee* (Joplin, MO: College Press, 1996), 114.

6. Ibid.

7. Leonard Sweet, *Aqua Church* (Loveland, CO: Group Publishing, 1999), 27.

8. See "One-In-A-Million," *The Connection* (Feb. 27, 2001): 9A.

9. Cacioppo, "Why Loneliness Is Bad for Your Health."

10. Sweet, *Aqua Church*, 28.

11. Henri Nouwen, quoted in Edythe Draper, *Draper's Book of Quotations for the Christian World* (Wheaton: Tyndale, 1992), entry 10545.

12. Dietrich Bonhoeffer, *A Testament to Freedom: The Essential Writings of Dietrich Bonhoeffer*, ed. Geffrey B. Kelly and F. Burton Nelson (San Francisco: Harper, 1990), 350–51.

Chapter 3 Hands in the Cookie Jar

1. Paul Deussen, quoted in Hans Kung, *Does God Exist? An Answer for Today*, trans. Edward Quinn (New York: Crossroad Publishing, 1978), 352.

2. C. S. Lewis, quoted in Draper, *Draper's Book of Quotations for the Christian World*, entry 10419.

3. Garrison Keillor, quoted in John Ortberg, "What IBM Taught Me about Repentance," *Christianity Today* (Aug. 12, 1993): 37.

4. Henri Nouwen, *The Return of the Prodigal Son: A Story of Homecoming* (New York: Image, 1994), 100–101.

Chapter 4 Riding the Roller Coaster

1. Personal interview.

2. Ibid.

3. Ibid.

4. Ibid.

5. Ibid.

6. Philip Yancey, *Where Is God When It Hurts?* (Grand Rapids: Zondervan, 1990), 77.

7. Joni Eareckson Tada, "Life Is Hard, but God Is Good," audiotape of a message presented for *Preaching Today*, no. 209 (Carol Stream, IL: Preaching Today, 2000).

8. Henri Nouwen, quoted in Draper, *Draper's Book of Quotations for the Christian World*, entry 1513.

9. Personal interview.

10. Ibid.

Chapter 5 Can't Get No Satisfaction

1. Despair, Inc., "Demotivators," http://www.despair.com/viewall.html.

2. Peggy Noonan, quoted in Gary Moore, *Ten Golden Rules for Financial Success* (Grand Rapids: Zondervan, 1996), 185–86.

3. *Forrest Gump*, directed by Robert Zemeckis (1994; Paramount Pictures, 2001), DVD.

4. Quoted in Scott Wenig, "Hide and Seek," audiotape of a message presented for *Preaching Today* (Carol Stream, IL: Preaching Today, 2001).

5. Henri Nouwen, *Life of the Beloved* (New York: Crossroads, 1992), 21.

6. B. B. Warfield, *The Person and Work of Christ*, ed. Samuel G. Craig (Philadelphia: Presbyterian & Reformed Publishing, 1950), 96.

7. Charles Milak, quoted in Draper, *Draper's Book of Quotations for the Christian World*, entry 10807.

8. *Forbes*, quoted in Moore, *Ten Golden Rules for Financial Success*, 187.

9. Andy Stanley, panel discussion, Catalyst Conference (Alpharetta, GA: North Point Community Church), October 24, 2002.

10. Frederick Buechner, *Peculiar Treasures: A Biblical Who's Who* (New York: Harper & Row, 1979), 180.

11. Deion Sanders, *Power, Money & Sex: How Success Almost Ruined My Life* (Dallas: Word, 1998), 194.

Chapter 6 Hugging the Cactus

1. "Robert Downey Jr. Asks for Forgiveness for Mel Gibson," YouTube video, 2:04, posted by telegraphtv on Oct. 18, 2011, http://www.youtube.com/watch?v=_AAJuynxnTQ.

2. Mark Moore, *The Chronological Life of Christ Volume 2: From Galilee to Glory* (Joplin, MO: College Press, 1997), 267–68.

3. William D. Edwards et al., "On the Physical Death of Jesus Christ," *Journal of the American Medical Association* 255, no. 11 (March 21, 1986): 1457.

4. Thomas Cahill, *The Desire for the Everlasting Hills* (New York: Nan A. Talese Publishing, 1999), 285.

5. Ibid., 285–86.

6. *The Voyager's Collection Catalog*, 80.

7. Friedrich Nietzsche, *Beyond Good and Evil: Prelude to a Philosophy of the Future*, trans. Walter Kaufmann (New York: Vintage, 1996), 60.

8. John Stott, *The Cross of Christ* (Downers Grove, IL: InterVarsity Press, 1986), 212.

9. Kahlil Gibran, *The Treasury of Kahlil Gibran*, trans. Anthony Rizcallah Ferris, ed. Martin Wolf (Secaucus, NJ: The Citadel Press, 1979), 152–56.

10. Leo Tolstoy, quoted in *A Diary of Readings*, trans. Aylmer Maude, ed. John Baillie (New York: Collier Books, 1955), 63.

11. Linda Storm, *Karla Faye Tucker Set Free: Life and Faith on Death Row* (Colorado Springs: Waterbrook Press, 2000), 15–16.

12. Ibid., 24–25.

13. John Piper, *Future Grace* (Sisters, OR: Multnomah, 1995), 111–18.

14. Ibid., 112.

15. Barry McMurtrie introduced me to the concept of the church as a spiritual M*A*S*H unit.

16. Personal interview.

17. Ibid.

Chapter 7 The Wow Factor

1. Theodoret, quoted in *Ancient Christian Commentary on Scripture: Galatians, Ephesians, Philippians*, New Testament, vol. 8., ed. Mark J. Edwards (Downers Grove, IL: InterVarsity Press, 1999), 271.

2. Søren Kierkegaard, *Purity of Heart Is to Will One Thing*, trans. Douglas Steele (New York: Harper & Row, 1948), 151.

3. Personal interview.

4. Ibid.

5. Ibid.

6. Personal interview.

7. Ibid.

8. Ibid.

9. Ibid.

Conclusion

1. Brennan Manning, *All Is Grace: A Ragamuffin Memoir* (Colorado Springs: David C. Cook, 2011), 177.

2. Ibid.

Jud Wilhite is an author, a speaker, and senior pastor of Central Christian Church, a church founded in Las Vegas with campuses in multiple states. Central is recognized as one of the largest and fastest growing churches in America. A recent study revealed that 98 percent of people surveyed at Central said God "saved their lives" through the community of the church. In partnership with God Behind Bars, Central has also innovated multisite church campuses inside prisons in strategic states.

Jud is the author of several books including *Torn, Throw It Down,* and *Uncensored Grace.* He and his wife Lori have two kids and live in the Las Vegas area.